SAVE $50,000
ON YOUR NEW HOME

SAVE $50,000
ON YOUR NEW HOME
Yes!
You Can Be Your Own
General Contractor

WILLIAM J. MOLLOY

New York • Chichester • Weinheim • Brisbane • Singapore • Toronto

Copyright © 1997 by William J. Molloy
Published by John Wiley & Sons, Inc.

Library of Congress Cataloging-in-Publication Data:

Molloy, William J., 1947–
    Save $50,000 on your new home . yes! you can be your own general
contractor / by William J. Molloy.
        p.   cm.
    Includes index.
    ISBN 0-471-15562-4 (pbk.   alk. paper)
    1. House construction—Amateurs' manuals.   2. Building—
Superintendence—Amateurs' manuals.   3. Contractors—Selection
and appointment—Amateurs' manuals.   I. Title.
TH4815.M65   1997
690'.837—dc20   96-40985
                                                              CIP

Printed in the United States of America

10 9 8 7 6 5 4 3 2 1

CONTENTS

CONTENTS

CONTENTS

CONTENTS

Illustrations

ILLUSTRATIONS

Tables

TABLES

Acknowledgments

I would like to thank all who, through the years, have helped to make this and future books a reality: Thomas and Ethel Molloy and Pat, Al, and Linda Catalina of Vista, California; my wife and better half, Carolyn Molloy, who has always encouraged me; my handsome son Mark Molloy of Pound Ridge, New York; and my best friend Marilyn Molloy of Pound Ridge, New York. I thank Paul Burger, Republic Mortgage, and Greg J. Moore, architect, both of Las Vegas, Nevada, for their expert help. To all home buyers, who deserve the best advice and a chance to fulfill their dreams, and most of all to Mike Hamilton, senior editor for John Wiley & Sons, Inc., for helping to fulfill my dreams—thank you.

Preface

Congratulations! You are about to make your dream come true!

You have driven the required 2,000 miles to check out the resale-home market. You have visited homes you could not afford and would not buy the ones you could afford. You have visited the new-home developments, and the price was not right, or the floor plans were not right, or the location or the exterior or the lot size or something else was not right. So here you are, thinking that the only way for you to achieve your goal of the right house at an affordable price is to try to build it yourself.

Well, you are right! Can you build you own home without any knowledge of the construction business? Yes! Can you build it without experiencing a horror story? Yes! Can you stay in control and not be overwhelmed? Yes! Can this be true? Yes!

How? If you could save the broker's 10-percent commission when buying the land, purchase the building materials for as much as 30 percent off the retail price, save almost 50 percent in bank closing costs, and not have to pay the full builder profit, do you think you would save money?

If the land cost were $50,000, the broker's commission would be $5,000. If the cost of house materials averaged about $70,000 and you saved 30 percent, you would save $21,000. If you limited your closing costs to one closing instead of two, you would save about $12,000 on the average house. If you saved the builder's markup, you would save at least another $30,000.

If I add all those savings, I get $68,000 saved. Even if I make mistakes, I should be able to save at least $50,000 by building my own home, shouldn't I?

Read this book!

Introduction:
How This Book Is Different

This book is not intended to make you into a professional home builder. On the contrary; it will allow you to become an armchair general contractor even if you have never picked up a hammer. How can this be, you ask?

More than 25 years ago, with sales experience under my belt, I jumped into the general contracting business and became an armchair builder. Since that time I have been involved in buying, building, or selling more than 100 homes and buying or selling more than 150 building lots. My first book, *The Complete Home Buyer's Bible*, published by John Wiley & Sons, New York, guides the buyer easily through the complicated maze of acquiring an existing home by providing a step-by-step process with explanations of the specialized terminology. This book goes much further and allows the home buyer to design, finance, and actually participate in the creation of that dream home.

You don't have to know all the technical aspects of construction. You simply need to know how to hire the right people to do the job—to do it right, within your budget, and on time.

This book takes you from the initial idea to the structuring of the financing, from obtaining the building plans and permits to finding the building lot, from negotiations with the bank and the lot owner to negotiations with the contractors. This book is a reference guide. Take it with you throughout the process, and refer to it as the need arises. Refer to the index in the back to locate terms you will be exposed to. Do not be afraid to interrupt a conversation to look up the meaning of a word or phrase. Professional people just love to dazzle you with footwork and 10-dollar words. If you do not understand, ask for an explanation. If you do not receive a satisfying explanation, *you* explain that if you are not comfortable with the terminology and the process, you will go somewhere else.

The key ingredient is that *you are in control of the entire process*. This book tells you how.

How Much House
Can I Afford?

Calculate Your Financial Net Worth

Before you begin this exciting journey, you need to understand your financial strengths. There is no point in spending weeks of your valuable free time poring over magazines and looking at house styles and sizes only to find out later than you can't afford to build your dream home. You need to calculate your net worth to see how far a lender will go to finance your dream. Most people are surprised to find out how much they are actually worth. I mention *lender* and not *bank* because banks are not the only sources of funds. The lender will be the entity that actually lends you the money.

Because you will be seeking a mortgage for a single-family home, you should approach your local *savings bank*. Most savings banks are required, by state and federal law, to lend a certain amount within the local community for home mortgages. If you know someone in your target area who can recommend a local bank, you will save valuable time.

An alternative to a savings bank is a mortgage banker (not the same as a mortgage broker). Companies that supply mortgages advertise in local papers or Yellow Pages. Commercial banks usually charge higher fees and

Before you begin this exciting journey, you need to understand your financial strengths.

higher interest rates than savings banks because most of their customers are businesses.

Savings banks usually lend at lower rates than do commercial banks, and home mortgaging is a substantial part of their business. The savings bank is limited to loan criteria approved by its board of directors, and it only lends its own money.

A *mortgage broker* is an agent who has access not only to banks but to insurance companies, investor groups, federal funds, and a host of other sources. The broker cannot approve the loan; he or she can only try to place your loan with a lender.

Like a mortgage broker, a *mortgage banker* has access to many types of lenders. The main difference is that a mortgage banker is also a lender and has the ability to approve a loan application and commit the funds.

When you meet with prospective lenders—and you should meet with several to see what your options are—bring copies of the *plot plan* (the lot survey with the proposed improvements included) and the house *check print* (the initial sketch of the house design and floor plan) if you have them. These documents will save time and avoid guesswork.

When I started building new homes in 1973, I was still living in an apartment. My financial statement showed a lender that I could qualify on paper, but I had to use my meager cash reserves (I started with about $5,000) to operate my fledgling building business. I couldn't afford to build my own home and stay in business at the same time. When I reached the point where I could afford to build my own home, I made the same mistake most of my customers made. I bought housing magazines and looked at the fancy exteriors and vast floor plans with various built-in features. I fantasized about this huge house on the hill with a circular driveway and a three-car garage. The only problem was that I couldn't afford it. I checked my finances *after* I imagined my dream and, with great disappointment, scaled down the size, took out the built-ins, and decided that a two-car garage was enough.

It is crucial to understand your finances. Knowing your limitations now will save you disappointment and valuable time later. You can plan and dream realistically,

When I reached the point where I could afford to build my own home, I made the same mistake most of my customers made.

4

and believe me, it is more fun to know that what you are planning will come true. The following Personal Financial Statement, divided into four parts, will help you develop a realistic view of your finances. This form is similar to those the lenders use. I've provided sample numbers in certain categories to illustrate how the figures add together to show an actual net worth. Use your own numbers, and you will see how your financial picture comes together. The first section (Table 1.1) asks for personal information about the borrower.

The coapplicant section is for anyone who may offer to sign the financing agreements with you (cosign). Don't be shy. If you can't qualify on your own, don't be afraid to ask relatives or friends to help. If this is your first home, it will probably be the toughest to qualify for. If not having a coapplicant means you will not qualify for the loan, get a cosigner. Your goal is to build the home now and enjoy the benefits of home ownership. Do not let pride stand in your way. Time and again I have seen potential homeowners decide to wait to save more money instead of asking for help. By the time they had saved more money, material and land prices had increased, and they still couldn't afford to build. Interest rates change every day. Material and labor prices rarely decline, and if the area is active, you may not find that perfect building lot in the future. Grasp the opportunity

It is crucial to understand your finances. Knowing your limitations now will save you disappointment and valuable time later.

Don't be shy. If you can't qualify on your own, don't be afraid to ask relatives or friends to help.

TABLE 1.1 Personal Financial Statement (Section One)

Applicant	*Coapplicant*
Applicant's name	Coapplicant's name
Home address	Home address
Home phone (Date of birth)	Home phone (Date of birth)
Social Security number	Social Security number
Employer	Employer
Business phone (No. of years)	Business phone (No. of years)
Title/position	Title/position
Previous employer & phone	Previous employer & phone
Title/position	Title/position
Accountant's name & phone	Accountant's name & phone
Attorney's name & phone	Attorney's name & phone
Investment advisor & phone	Investment advisor & phone

TABLE 1.2   Personal Financial Statement (Section Two)

Annual income		Annual expenditures	
Salary (applicant) (combined)	$35,000	Federal income and other taxes	$ 8,000
Salary (coapplicant)	$	State and other income taxes	$
Bonuses & commissions (applicant)	$	Rental payments; coop or condo maintenance	$ 6,000
Bonuses & commissions (coapplicant)	$	Mortgage payments	$
Partnership income	$	Property taxes	$
Rental income	$	Interest & principal payments on loans	$ 1,000
Interest income	$ 1,000	Insurance	$ 450
Dividend income	$	Payments on investments	$
Capital gains	$	Tuition	$ 1,200
Other investment income	$	Other living expenses	$
Other income (side jobs)	$ 4,200	Medical expenses	$
Total income $	$40,200	Total expenditures	$16,650

now and get it done. The next section of the financial statement, in Table 1.2, deals with your present income and living expenses.

In Table 1.2, if you subtract total expenditures from total income, you will see a net income of $23,550. Include income of any kind, even baby-sitting income, as long as it is consistent income for one year. If you receive a dividend or interest from a bank account, include it. You need to show the lender your total picture of income from all available sources. You want the net income number to be as large as possible. This number shows the lender how much net income you have to qualify for the mortgage. However, you are worth more than that. You will be asked for other information, such as any changes in job status expected in the next 12 months or whether you have ever experienced a bankruptcy. Just answer honestly. Table 1.3. provides for additional information to calculate your net worth.

You didn't know you were worth that much, did you? Again, put down as much as you can. If you own stocks or bonds (marketable securities), find out their worth and include them. Also include securities if they are nonmarketable or are in a trust or in the form of

TABLE 1.3 Personal Financial Statement (Section Three)

Assets		Liabilities	
Cash on hand and in banks	$ 20,000	Life insurance loans	$
Cash value of life insurance	$ 25,000	Bank loans	$
Marketable securities	$ 5,000	Credit card debts	$ 2,500
Accounts receivable	$	Taxes owed	$ 6,500
Real estate for personal use	$	Personal loans	$ 400
Investment property	$	Auto loans	$ 8,500
Ownership of business assets	$ 7,500	Other debts	$ 2,000
Automobiles (s)	$ 2,500		$
Recreational vehicles	$		$
Personal effects	$ 20,000		$
Retirement plans	$ 15,000		$
Other assets	$ 5,000	Total liabilities	$ 19,900
		Net worth	$ 80,100
Total assets	$100,000	Total liabilities & net worth	$119,900

shares you may own in a small company. If someone owes you money for a service performed or an item purchased, put that sum under "Accounts receivable." If you have any real-estate investments or own a share of a vacation package, include that information on the appropriate line. What is your automobile worth over and above the bank loan? If you own recreational vehicles or equipment (even golf clubs have value), include these. Your personal effects have value. You may own TVs, VCRs, tape players, refrigerators, washers, dryers, jewelry, fur coats, furniture, computers, clothes, office equipment, computer programs, and dishware—everything has value. If you are invested in a 401K or IRA retirement program, include this information as well.

You may be surprised at the final number when you finish adding up all that you have. The lender will discount some of the items—such as the clothes on your back—as not applicable, but the lender asked for the numbers, and you want your financial picture to look its best.

Although lenders look at numbers, they are still people. First impressions are lasting impressions, and I have always provided the highest possible net worth

TABLE 1.4 Personal Financial Statement (Section Four)

Cash on hand and in banks

Bank	Account type	Account no.	Date opened	Balance

Life insurance values

Company	Owner	Face amount	Cash value	Loans

Marketable securities: stocks, bonds, treasury bills

No. of shares	Description	Owner	Mkt. value	Restricted?

Nonmarketable securities

No. of shares	Description	Owner	Mkt. value	Restricted?

Accounts and notes receivable

Date	Due from	Original amount	Present value	Terms

Real estate for personal use

Address	% owned	Date purchased	Cost	Mkt. value

Real estate investments

Description	% owned	Date purchased	Cost	Mkt. value

Ownership of business assets

Bus. name	Bus. type	% owned	Cost	Mkt. value

Retirement plans: IRAs, keogh, profit sharing

Institution	Type of plan	Acct. no.	Beneficiary	Mkt. value

Loans owed to banks, brokers, finance companies

Owed to	Amount	Balance due	Date due	Purpose

when asked to fill out these forms. It is not my job to figure what is good for the lender; I want the loan.

The next question may be whether you are a coguarantor for another loan or an endorser for any other debts for someone else. Are you liable for an apartment lease? Are there back taxes due? Answer these questions and go on. Table 1.4 shows how to back up the numbers provided in Tables 1.2 and 1.3.

Other information may be needed, but most of the forms are similar. The lender simply needs to know your ability to repay a loan and, in the event you default, the amount the lender can recover.

If you have had credit problems in the past, **do not** try to hide them. In this age of instant electronic information, your credit history is readily available. Lenders understand that things happen in life, and there are hundreds of formulas and criteria for writing loans for people who have had credit problems. I spoke with a loan officer in Las Vegas who recently had closed a loan for a couple with a prior bankruptcy and only $700 in cash to buy the house.

Organize Your Finances

Hold on! You're not ready to go out the door just yet. You need to draw on the information in Tables 1.1 through 1.4 to estimate your level of affordability by using the formulas provided in the following pages.

I strongly recommend that you go to several savings banks, mortgage brokers, and mortgage bankers to obtain the current interest rates and loan criteria. Savings banks generally loan at rates lower than those charged by commercial banks. However, banks are somewhat limited by their stockholders' requirements. Mortgage brokers have longer lists of lenders, but they are also limited because they are third parties, not actual lenders. Mortgage bankers may have the best of both worlds: They have many sources for funds combined with the ability actually to lend the money.

The financing, like the house and the land, must be packaged. You must find the building lot that comple-

First impressions are lasting impressions, and I have always provided the highest possible net worth when asked to fill out these forms.

If you have had credit problems in the past, do not try to hide them. In this age of instant electronic information, your credit history is readily available.

The lender must be able to package the financing into one loan for land acquisition, construction, and closing of the permanent loan in a single transaction.

ments the size and style of your home design and combine the elements into one project. The lender must be able to package the financing into one loan for land acquisition, construction, and closing of the permanent loan in a single transaction. I will cover the packaging of the entire project later in this chapter.

Take your time with the following formulas. Don't be intimidated if the calculation sounds complicated. It is complicated, but if I can do it, anyone can. If you can graduate high school or college, get a job, get married, and/or have children, you can do this. If you take into account all of the items people spend money on today—$100 sneakers, $1.25-per-gallon gasoline, and $15 movie tickets (not including the popcorn)—you may find that you make enough in gross income to qualify for the required loan. But can you realistically afford to make the payments? From Tables 1.1 through 1.4 you have an idea of your financial net worth, but lenders will use your gross and net income numbers actually to calculate your level of affordability.

The best way to figure your ability to pay the mortgage is to work from a budget. Table 1.5 is an example of a typical monthly budget. Make up one of your own, using your own monthly living expenses. Be honest with your budget—you will use real dollars when the payment is due.

You were surprised to learn your actual net worth, and you may also be surprised to learn what your living expenses amount to. Check to see where you can save money. If you are not reading that magazine, why continue to pay for it? If you don't use the club benefits, why pay the dues? Try to save wherever you can. The more you save monthly, the more house you can afford.

Try to save wherever you can. The more you save monthly, the more house you can afford.

Before we enter the maze of numbers, you need to understand some of the terminology and criteria the lender will use to formulate a plan to finance your dream. There are hundreds of ways to qualify for financing. However, for the purposes of this book, we will use the formulas the lender would employ to qualify you for a *conventional loan.* A conventional loan is a loan that does not require insurance to cover amounts that exceed 80 percent of the *appraised value* of the *total package.* This is known as the *loan-to-value ratio.*

HOW MUCH HOUSE CAN I AFFORD?

TABLE 1.5   Monthly Budget Outline

Monthly budget outline for house purchase

Rent	$
Utilities	$
Groceries	$
Clothes	$
Car payments	$
Auto fuel	$
Auto insurance	$
Life insurance	$
Health insurance	$
Retirement funds	$
Loan repayments	$
Credit cards	$
Work-related (food, child care, dues)	$
Medical expenses	$
Entertainment	$
Personal care (haircuts, laundry, stylist)	$
Magazine & newspaper subscriptions	$
Home maintenance	$
Contributions & gifts	$
Club memberships	$
Total monthly living express	$

An appraiser is a professional hired by the lender, and paid by you, to provide an estimate of value (*appraised value*) of the land together with the improvements for the *total package* or *package price*. The improvements are anything that you will do to add value to the property such as building the house, laying the driveway, installing the water/well and sewer/septic systems, and landscaping. For example, if your building lot price is $25,000 and the cost of building the home and completing the package with all improvements is $75,000, then the total package price will be $100,000. Under conventional financing requirements, the lender will commit to lend 80 percent or $80,000 (loan to value) of that amount.

As of this writing, there are 95-percent loans available for new construction. Such a loan would only require you to put down a maximum of 5 percent of the cost of the total package. For the purposes of this chapter, I will use the 80-percent conventional formula and explain the requirements for the 95-percent ratio later in the chapter.

There are other lower-interest housing loan programs, such as Federal Housing Authority (FHA) or Veterans Administration (VA) guaranteed or insured loans, but they do not involve new construction. However, you may find that your state offers programs for lower-interest loans that also cover new construction. Ask your lender if such financing is available in your area.

How Much Can I Borrow?

We are going to work with several mathematical formulas, the same formulas the lenders use, to calculate the amount of mortgage you qualify for and your ability to make the monthly payments. You need to qualify for the total amount of the *permanent mortgage* (end loan) before you can structure the construction financing.

To work through these formulas, you will need a pad of paper, a pencil, and a calculator. Take your time. Read each portion several times until you are comfortable with the formulas. It is not as hard as it looks.

You have calculated your net worth to show a lender that you are a good financial risk. Your budget shows you where you can save and how much you have available to spend for your mortgage. However, the lender will still qualify you by using a percentage of a *gross monthly income* (GMI) formula. You have figured your gross annual income by following the example in Table 1.2. Simply divide your gross annual income by 12 to determine your GMI. The sample numbers in Table 1.2 show a gross annual income of $40,200. The GMI would be $3,350 ($40,200 / 12 = $3,350).

Even though a myriad of mortgage rates exist, most lenders will first qualify you at the standard 30-year fixed-rate formula before getting creative with numbers. The lender will use one of two basic formulas, with debt figured as 36 percent of GMI or, if you have no other debts (lucky you), as 28 percent of GMI. If you have other debts such as car payments, college loans, or debts that require more than 10 months to repay, the lender will use

Even though a myriad of mortgage rates exist, most lenders will first qualify you at the standard 30-year fixed-rate formula before getting creative with numbers.

12

HOW MUCH HOUSE CAN I AFFORD?

TABLE 1.6   Calculating 28 Percent of GMI

Gross monthly income = $3,350 × 28% =	$938
Estimated monthly property tax	−100
Estimated monthly insurance cost	−30
Monthly amount available for principal and interest	$808

the 36-percent formula. The difference between 28 percent and 36 percent, or 8 percent, is to be used to reduce your debts.

The income percentages are based on your ability to repay the sum of four separate expenses: principal, interest, taxes, and insurance (PITI). The amount you will borrow is known as the *principal* amount. *Interest* is charged on the principal amount borrowed. You will owe *taxes* on the property, and the total package must be *insured* against damage, theft, and personal injury. To qualify for the loan, you must have a gross monthly income that enables you to pay 28 percent of it toward PITI if you have no other debts that extend more than 10 months or 36 percent if you do have such debts.

Study the examples in Table 1.6 to see how the first debt figure works.

After deducting taxes and insurance from 28 percent of your GMI, you have $808 to spend for your mortgage. If, like most of us, you have debts, the balance will be different, as Table 1.7 shows.

You can see how the dollar amounts change with the different formulas. You now know how much you can afford monthly for either formula, but how much can you borrow?

TABLE 1.7   Calculating 36 Percent of GMI

Gross monthly income = $3,350 × 36% =	$1,206
Estimated monthly property tax	−100
Estimated monthly insurance cost	−30
Estimated monthly car payment	−150
Estimated monthly student loan payment	−50
Monthly amount available for principal and interest	$876

TABLE 1.8 Finding a Constant Number

Interest rates	5 Years	10 Years	15 Years	20 Years	25 Years	30 Years
5%	18.88	10.61	7.91	6.60	5.85	5.37
5-1/2%	19.11	10.86	8.18	6.88	6.15	5.68
6%	19.34	11.11	8.44	7.17	6.45	6.00
6-1/2%	19.57	11.36	8.72	7.46	6.76	6.33
7%	19.81	11.62	8.99	7.76	7.07	6.66
7-1/2%	20.04	11.88	9.28	8.06	7.39	7.00
8%	20.28	12.14	9.56	8.37	7.72	7.34
8-1/2%	20.52	12.40	9.85	8.68	8.06	7.69
9%	20.76	12.67	10.15	9.00	8.40	8.05
9-1/2%	21.01	12.94	10.45	9.33	8.74	8.41
10%	21.25	13.22	10.75	9.66	9.09	8.78
10-1/2%	21.50	13.50	11.06	9.99	9.45	9.15
11%	21.75	13.78	11.37	10.33	9.81	9.53
11-1/2%	22.00	14.06	11.69	10.67	10.17	9.91
12%	22.25	14.35	12.01	11.02	10.54	10.29
12-1/2%	22.50	14.64	12.33	11.37	10.91	10.68
13%	22.76	14.94	12.66	11.72	11.28	11.07
13-1/2%	23.01	15.23	12.99	12.08	11.66	11.46
14%	23.27	15.53	13.32	12.44	12.04	11.85

Every mortgage is based on a repayment schedule that shows the number of dollars required to repay the number of dollars borrowed (represented in thousands of dollars).

Every mortgage is based on a repayment schedule that shows the number of dollars required to repay the number of dollars borrowed (represented in thousands of dollars). The amount needed to repay the loan is known as a *constant* number. Study Table 1.8 to see how to find a constant number. The top row shows the number of years the borrower needs to repay the loan; the first column on the left shows the desired interest rate. Slide your finger over to the "30 Years" column; then slide your finger down to the "7%" row. Your finger should be resting on the constant number 6.66. Remember, mortgage repayments are calculated on dollars per thousand. The 6.66 number represents the amount of principal and interest ($6.66) required to repay $1,000 for 30 years at 7 percent interest.

To find out how much borrowing power your available funds give you, convert the constant number to a fraction. The constant for 30 years at 7 percent is 6.66. Change 6.66 to .00666 by moving the decimal point to the left of the number and adding two zeroes. Now take the amount available from Table 1.6 (without debts = $808), and divide that number by the constant fraction of .00666. You will see that, for a monthly principal and interest payment of $808, you can repay a mortgage of $121,321.32 over 30 years at 7 percent interest ($808/ .00666 = $121,321.32).

Now look back at Table 1.7, based on the formula that allows for debts. It shows $876 available for principal and interest payments. With this figure, you could afford to borrow $131,531.53, depending upon your credit status, work history, and ability to complete the project.

You will be required to pay the difference between the total package cost and the maximum mortgage amount in cash. If the total package cost is $151,531.53, you will have to come up with 20 percent in cash *plus* the cost of closing the loan with the lender. Closing costs vary from 4 to 5 percent of the cost of the loan in the western states to 8 to 9 percent of the loan in the East. For example, for a $100,000 loan in Las Vegas, Nevada, your closing costs would be about $4,000 plus the down payment. *Do not panic if you do not have the 20 percent in cash. I will cover creative financing and loan closing costs later in this chapter.* Stay with the simple formulas for now to get an understanding of the process.

Check the current interest rates available for *conventional loans.* Remember, FHA and VA loans are not currently available for new construction. Also, you will see interest rates jumping all over the pages of your local newspaper. *Do not* target the lowest rate you can find— usually a one-year adjustable-rate mortgage (ARM)— and start planning that mansion you always wanted. Lenders will always qualify you first on the basis of a 30-year fixed-rate loan at current conventional rates. Ask your lenders what the current conventional rate is, and use that in your calculations for now. Be realistic and (KISS) keep it simple.

Now that you think the calculation is easy, we will create more confusion. Using Table 1.8 to find the constant number is simple, but what if the quoted rates are not in even numbers—for instance, $7^3/8$ percent or $6^5/8$ percent? Table 1.9 shows how to convert these fractions to decimal fractions to make the task easier. Don't worry about getting the numbers exactly right. When you meet

Do not target the lowest rate you can find—usually a one-year adjustable-rate mortgage (ARM)— and start planning that mansion you always wanted. Lenders will always qualify you first on the basis of a 30-year fixed-rate loan at current conventional rates.

15

TABLE 1.9 Fractions Converted to Decimal Fractions

1/4	0.25
3/8	0.38
1/2	0.50
5/8	0.63
3/4	0.75
7/8	0.88

with the lender, you will be able to discuss more concrete figures.

To keep it simple, just use the constant number chart in Table 1.8 to derive an estimate for your mortgage. Check your personal budget and find the balance available after expenses to make mortgage payments. Check the current interest rate and the desired number of years to repay, find the constant number, and do the math. You now have a good idea of your level of affordability. Before we discuss construction financing, you need to know more about mortgages.

What Is a Mortgage?

Mortgage *is a combination of two French words,* mort, *which means dead, and* gage, *which means pledge and was used in Anglo-Saxon times.*

Mortgage is a combination of two French words, *mort,* which means dead, and *gage,* which means pledge and was used in Anglo-Saxon times. The *mortgage note* is your agreement to the terms of the loan, and the *mortgage bond* is your guarantee (promise) that you will repay the debt according to the terms in the mortgage note.

The *conventional* mortgage is a loan that does not require any further guarantee or insurance of repayment beyond the mortgage bond and note. (Loans that do not need a repayment guarantee from FHA or VA are called conventional loans.) The loan is for a maximum of 80 percent of the *appraised value* of the total package. Here is a simplified example: If the building lot purchase price is $20,000 and the cost of building the home is $80,000, the total package price will be $100,000. If the bank will lend 80 percent of that package, your mortgage amount will be $80,000. You will need to supply cash for the balance of the package cost and the closing costs.

Creative Financing

We have been using the conventional loan method to calculate the funds available to build, but there may be other methods your lender may offer or accept.

If you do not qualify for the 80 percent loan-to-value 30-year fixed-rate loan, or if you find yourself short on cash, ask the lender if it would consider qualifying you at the Adjustable-Rate Mortgage (ARM) rate for the permanent (*take-out*) loan. You will use a *construction loan* to build the project, and the *permanent loan* will pay off (take out) the construction loan when the project is finished. I will cover the construction loan in Chapter 9.

ARM interest rates are usually much lower than current fixed rates and should enable you to qualify for more financing. The lender might agree to offer you a 90-percent or even a 95-percent loan package. The amount will depend heavily on your credit record, your job stability, your income, and your ability to convince the lender that you can complete the project.

Any loan that exceeds the conventional loan requirements of 80 percent loan to value will require the amount exceeding 80 percent to be insured or guaranteed. For example, if your package cost totals $100,000, a conventional loan will cover 80 percent of that amount, or $80,000. If you don't have $20,000 for the balance plus the closing costs, you may instead need to borrow 90 percent loan to value, or $90,000. The amount that exceeds the 80 percent loan-to-value requirement—in this case, the additional $10,000—must have insurance or a guarantee to the lender that the amount will be repaid no matter what happens with the project. FHA and VA do not get involved with new custom homes, but *private mortgage insurance* (PMI) companies do. PMI will insure the amount that exceeds the 80 percent criterion and allow the lender to commit more money to you.

PMI fees are calculated on the total amount borrowed. The exact formula used to calculate the cost of the PMI premium depends on the amount and type of mortgage you apply for. An example for a 30-year fixed-rate permanent loan at a loan-to-value ratio of 95 percent of market value would be similar to the example in Table 1.10.

Any loan that exceeds the conventional loan requirements of 80 percent loan to value will require the amount exceeding 80 percent to be insured or guaranteed.

TABLE 1.10   Calculating PMI

Market value estimate	$100,000
95% Mortgage available	$95,000
Conventional 80% loan	$80,000
Conventional loan exceeded by	$15,000
Current formula = .0078 × $95,000	$741
$741 divided by 12 months = (per month)	$62

Another way to use less cash is to ask the lot owner to participate.

The most successful formula I offered to an owner was a 10–40–50 deal.

With this loan you will be required to pay an additional $62 per month until the additional $15,000 of the mortgage is repaid. When you reach the 80 percent loan-to-value stage, you can cancel your PMI by notifying your lender. *Don't forget to cancel the PMI.* Many buyers do forget, and the PMI companies continue to collect the money.

You must have enough cash available for a down payment on the building lot, deposits with the contractors, and the closing costs for the financing. In the Southwest, because of the current strong economies, lenders are offering 90 percent loan-to-value loans *that cover the purchase of the building lot and all closing costs.* You only need 10 percent of the total package in cash.

Another way to use less cash is to ask the lot owner to participate. This is usually a difficult proposition because of the landowner's own need for the money or a simple reluctance to get involved in the risk of your project. When I entered the building business in the 1970s, I had about $5,000 in cash and a lot of chutzpah. I watched what other builders were doing and learned that, with a little luck and a lot of tap dancing, you can convince the lot owner to help out.

The most successful formula I offered to an owner was a 10–40–50 deal. I would pay the owner 10 percent of the purchase price as a down payment on the land on contract. I would begin construction of the house, and when I closed the construction mortgage, I would pay the owner an additional 40 percent of the land price. The 50-percent balance would be paid when I closed the permanent mortgage at completion of the project. The beauty of that formula was that the only cash needed to complete the project was the 10 percent cash for the lot; I used the lender's money for the balance of the project. But remember, whatever you borrow will have to be repaid. For example, say that you have $15,000 in cash to play with, and the building lot price is $50,000. You offer the owner 10 percent, or $5,000, in cash on contract, and 40 percent, or $20,000, when the house is under roof; you close the construction loan and pay the balance of $25,000 when you close the *end loan*. That leaves you with $10,000 to use for contractor deposits, lender fees, professional fees, and emergencies. If you don't know the contractors you will be hiring, they may also ask for small advance deposits to ensure their payment. I will cover buying land and dealing with contractors in future chapters.

The advantage of this formula for you is obvious. The disadvantage for the lot owner is more dramatic, and it is the reason most owners will not participate in such a transaction. The lot owner simply wants to sell. An owner who agrees to take the money in increments must also agree to subordinate his or her interests to the lender's mortgage. *The lender will always be first in line.* You may have heard the terms *first mortgage, second mortgage,* and so on. The *first mortgagee* is always the first to be repaid in the event of a *foreclosure*. The *mortgagee* is the lender, and the *mortgagor* is the borrower. If you *default* on the terms of the financing, the lender will file to foreclose the loan and take the property. The lender will either complete the project and sell it or simply sell it to get the money back. You will be responsible to pay for any deficits. The second mortgagee is next in line, and so on down to the last creditor. The first mortgagee is only interested in recovering his or her own investment and is in control of the auction process. The second mortgagee may or may not recover any money; that is the main reason most property owners will not *hold paper* on a transaction, especially if they have to subordinate to a lender.

You will have to sell your plan to the lot owner in the same way you sold it to the lender. If you have other assets to pledge against the owner's participation, such as stocks, bonds, other real estate, or a cosigner—anything to make the landowner feel comfortable—use it. If you are short on cash, you don't have many options. If you have the cash, buy the lot.

The lender will always be first in line.

As previously mentioned, the lender will finance from 80 percent to 90 percent of the package, not including closing costs and professional fees. One of those fees will be for an architect, if you hire one, and will run from $500 to $2,500, depending on the size and detail of the house plans. You will also need a surveyor ($500 to $1,500) and/or an engineer ($500 to $1,500). Closing costs will run from 4 percent to 8 percent of the mortgage cost, depending on your target area. For example, let's assume that you're in a western state, your package costs $100,000, and the lender will finance 80 percent of that amount. You will need at least $20,000 in cash plus at least 4 percent, or $4,000, for closing costs plus $2,500 or more for building plans, professional fees, permit fees, and contractor deposits. You will also need money for a deposit on the lot. If you have $30,000 to play with, there's no problem, but if you don't, you need to become more creative. You will see how to leverage the package in Chapters 5 and 9 on buying the building lot and structuring the financing.

Now that you know your financial strengths, you can proceed to put the package together. But first, go to a local copy center and have business cards printed. You want to present yourself as someone with a serious intent to build a house. Everyone you meet will form an opinion about you within the first 30 seconds after initial contact. If you offer a business card with your handshake, you will present a positive image. Your contacts will also have

You will see how to leverage the package in Chapters 5 and 9 on buying the building lot and structuring the financing.

TABLE 1.11 Sample Business Card

Robert Smith
General Contractor
333 Anywhere Street
P.O. Box 000
Las Vegas, NV 89119
Home: 702-555-0000
Fax: 702-555-1111

your name and information so they can return calls. A simple card printed with black ink on a white background is inexpensive. It might look like the sample in Table 1.11.

    With your own business card, you will come across as a person ready and willing to do business. Always present yourself in a positive way, and never lie. If you don't know what you're talking about, you will be embarrassed when you are found out. If you don't know something, say so and ask for advice. You will find that almost everyone is willing to help.

Always present yourself in a positive way, and never lie.

CHAPTER
2

Do I Need
Professional Help?

Do I Need an Attorney?

If this is the first time you are buying real estate, it would make sense to secure as much protection as possible by hiring the professionals who can provide you with the answers you need.

If you have experience in buying land and negotiating with contractors, landowners, and lenders, the answer is no, you don't need an attorney. If you're new to these areas, it is wise to consult with an attorney before you begin the process.

First, find an attorney who specializes in real estate. Second, find a real-estate attorney who will help you make your dream come true. Let me qualify this statement. From more than 25 years of experience in this business, I have concluded that there are two basic types of real-estate attorneys: the *deal maker* and the *deal breaker*.

The deal maker takes the time to explain what a contract's legal language really means to you. The deal breaker assumes that you are not intelligent enough to understand these terms and doesn't bother. The deal maker returns your calls and is sympathetic to your concerns; the deal breaker does not and is not. The deal maker follows the progress of the project and files the required papers with the appropriate people when needed; the deal breaker does not. The deal maker will

From more than 25 years of experience in this business, I have concluded that there are two basic types of real-estate attorneys: the deal maker and the deal breaker.

compromise during negotiations to bring the transaction to a mutually beneficial conclusion. The deal breaker inserts difficult terms into the transaction to create the impression of earning his or her fee by protecting you; actually, he or she is jeopardizing the transaction by making the terms more difficult than is necessary. The deal maker usually has a pleasant demeanor and shares in your excitement. The deal breaker is always too busy to take the time. The deal maker is friendly and professional; the deal breaker is arrogant and aloof.

Find a deal maker. When you go to the town or city where you intend to build your new home, ask everyone you meet to recommend a good attorney. Usually, real-estate people cannot recommend other professionals to you unless they offer several names. They can however, tell you who their own attorneys are without formally recommending them.

When you find an attorney, ask him for the names and addresses of several past customers. An attorney who has nothing to hide will offer you several names. If the attorney says that's confidential, find another one. Check him out: Ask lenders, insurance people, anyone else who might know his work. You should be able to tell very quickly whether your prospective attorney is a deal maker or a deal breaker.

Do I Need an Engineer?

Do you need an engineer? Yes! You will find one the same way you found an attorney. Talk to people on construction sites. Call builders and ask for their recommendations. Ask your attorney and your lender. Ask enough people and you will have several names.

The engineer is the most valuable professional in this business.

The engineer is the most valuable professional in this business. She is the one who will tell you whether your chosen building lot has problems or requires expensive corrective work **before you buy the lot!**

If you are designing your own home instead of buying an over-the-counter set of plans, the engineer will help either to draw the plans or to find a qualified architect. If you have over-the-counter plans from a magazine, the engineer will be able to review those plans to make sure they conform to local building codes, redraw the areas that need changing, and stamp the plans with her license number for the building inspectors and the lender.

The engineer will be able to work with you from the beginning to ensure that the house size and style you desire will fit physically onto the building lot and also meet all requirements of local zoning ordinances.

The engineer can save you valuable time and money and should be chosen with care. Any professional must maintain enough business to make a profit. Engineers are no exception, but some of them take on too much work and do not complete what they have started. A certain number of jobs will not be completed because of many circumstances beyond their control. Often they will not receive payment for such projects. They must make up that lost revenue by taking on more work.

In such a case, the engineer becomes too busy to provide you with what you need to complete your one house. Make a contractual agreement spelling out exactly what is expected. The engineer expects to be paid on time, and you expect the work to be done on time. The engineer may ask for an advance payment. If so, ask her to spell out in writing what she will do to earn that and future payments and when the work will be done. Avoid the catch-22 that arises when she doesn't show up on time and you withhold payment, you withhold payment and she doesn't do the work, and so on and on. That does not get your house completed.

If you begin with a written agreement that spells out the responsibilities of both parties, you shouldn't have a problem. If either party meets his or her responsibilities and the other fails to perform, the other is liable for breach of contract. Discuss the terms of the agreement with your attorney, who may have experience with contractor agreements.

Do I Need a Surveyor?

Do you need a surveyor? Yes! The surveyor will work hand in hand with the engineer. The two may work out of the same office (or they may even be the same person). The surveyor measures the boundaries of the building lot

If you begin with a written agreement that spells out the responsibilities of both parties, you shouldn't have a problem.

to ensure that the lot lines and the deed description match. He will verify that the property you are purchasing is the property located on the specified site and that the size is correct.

The surveyor will also calculate the topography (elevations) of the lot to see where the high and low points are. Because water runs downhill, you want to build your new home on the higher elevation of the lot. If your new house is to be served by a septic system instead of a central sewer, you need to locate the septic fields on the lowest point of the lot to allow for gravity feed from the house to the septic system. Septic systems, wells, surveys, and topography plot plans are covered in later chapters.

The surveyor will locate the lot boundaries and elevations and give that information to the engineer. The engineer will take the information and design a plot plan that shows the projected locations for the house, the septic system or sewer lines, the well or water lines, the driveway, and any needed drainage work. Ask the engineer and the surveyor about their fee schedules. *Try to pay these professionals by the job and not by the hour.* Both should have enough experience in this area to be able to project their full costs (barring unforeseen problems) and to quote you complete job costs. If you pay by the hour, it will probably cost more because they have nothing to lose by taking longer to do the same work.

Make friends with these professionals. Treat them and their crews with respect; they can save you money if they like you.

Make friends with these professionals. Treat them and their crews with respect; they can save you money if they like you. Give their secretaries personal gifts, like a prepaid dinner for two (keep it simple; it's the thought that counts), and you will see your paperwork move along swiftly. If you have a problem on the job and need their services, you will want the work done as soon as possible, not with a delay of days or weeks due to their heavy workloads.

Time is money when you are financing the job, and you are paying for that privilege every minute of every day. For example, suppose that you have drawn $50,000 down on the construction loan, and the interest is calculated at 10 percent per year, or $5,000. Divide $5,000 by 365 days to get $13.70 per day in interest. If you draw $100,000, you pay $27.40 per day—that's $1.14 per hour. If the job sits idle for one week waiting for the engineer, according to this formula the delay would cost you $191.78 more in interest. If you have to wait for several contractors and material deliveries, it gets very expensive. Future chapters will say more about contractor agreements and ways to avoid delays.

CHAPTER
3

What Size and Style Home Do I Need?

What You Need versus What You Want

Now that you know your financial capabilities, you need to look into the size and style of home you want or need. What you need is a home that meets your needs for daily living and future growth. It might be a somewhat modest 1,500-square-foot home with three bedrooms, two bathrooms, and a two-car garage on a 10,000-square-foot ($1/4$-acre) lot. You might want a fireplace and ceramic tile for the kitchen counter and floor. This simple home could meet your daily needs for living space.

On the other hand, you may want to show off your success with a 2,000- to 3,000-square-foot southwestern-style ranch or a two-story New England–style colonial, with vaulted ceilings and a sunken living room and possibly a master bedroom suite with fireplace and sunken bathtub—all set on a 20,000-square-foot ($1/2$-acre) lot.

The choice depends on what you can afford to build. *Stay within your zone of affordability.* Don't become house poor because you want to keep up with the neighbors or show off for your friends. You will live in a fancy house with a big mortgage and high taxes and wonder when you last went to a movie. It is not worth it—and I speak from experience.

Stay within your zone of affordability. Don't become house poor because you want to keep up with the neighbors or show off for your friends.

When I built my own home in 1979, I bought all of the housing magazines. My wife and I cut out pictures of all the fancy options we wanted and created a scrapbook of *wants*. We forgot about our *needs*. Because I was a general contractor, I had access to many of these upgrade items, and I fell victim to the excitement. I built an impressive 3,700-square-foot custom Tudor-style split-level home with inlaid oak floors and gold-plated faucets to impress everyone. It was a beautiful house, and we loved it. The problem was that by the time the house was finished, the interest rates were climbing, and my business was slowing down. We had this big, gorgeous house and couldn't afford to furnish it. From the outside it looked wonderful. On the inside we had second-hand apartment furniture sitting on expensive carpet and tile.

With more common sense, I would have built a smaller home with less opulence, furnished it comfortably, and enjoyed it more. The local economy stayed soft for several years, and I was married to the house. My friends were out playing golf, and I was mowing two-acres of lawn. Never again!

Keep It Simple

House styles vary dramatically. Common sense will tell you which direction you must take.

House styles vary dramatically. Common sense will tell you which direction you must take. Most construction material today is precut to fit into the average home. The two-by-four stud comes in 8-foot lengths because the average ceiling height starts at 7 feet and 6 inches from the floor. Much will depend on local building codes and the construction techniques commonly used in your target area.

The construction industry is very labor sensitive. If the job takes longer to do, you will pay more to have it done. Simple! The standard (least expensive) ceiling height is 7 feet, 6 inches. If you want higher ceilings, which require more labor and material, the job will cost more.

When you see magazine pictures showing 20-foot-high ceilings with skylights and family rooms with sunken floor areas and built-in fireplaces, it all looks great, but it is not free. Look at Figure 3.1, which shows why atypical roof elevations will cost more than the stan-

WHAT SIZE AND STYLE HOME DO I NEED?

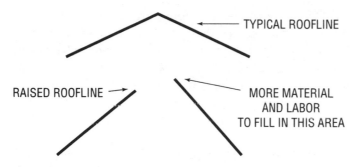

FIGURE 3.1   Typical and raised rooflines

dard roof. The least expensive roofline on a home is a straight $5/12$-pitch roof. This means that the roof elevation from the centerline will rise 5 inches higher for every foot in width from the center to the edge of the roof. It is a very easy and inexpensive roof to build.

When you raise the roofline, you need to fill that area with more material, which means that more labor is required and the job costs more to build. When you get into vaulted ceilings and steep-pitched rooflines, the cost continues to climb.

Visit New-Home Developments

The easiest way to find out about new construction costs in your chosen area is to visit new-home developments. Find developments that offer the style of home you desire. Walk through the models; get a feel for size and number of rooms. Find out the offerings of *upgrade* features such as fireplaces, ceramic countertops, and better carpets. Ask about the extra charges for those upgrades. Ask what the *standard* features are—for instance, hollow-core doors instead of raised-panel doors. Is the self-cleaning range standard or an upgrade? Ask the on-site agent or builder to explain the costs for the home you are viewing.

Ask if there are any additional charges for certain building lots. If a lot has a view or more trees or is next to a stream, a *premium* may be added to the standard lot

The easiest way to find out about new construction costs in your chosen area is to visit new-home developments. Walk through the models; get a feel for size and number of rooms.

cost. If the land and the house are combined into one price, tell the builder that you have a building lot and would like a price for just the completed *turnkey* house, without the land included. *Turnkey* means the entire completed project, including all soft costs such as professional fees, permits, and plans—virtually everything it takes to bring the project to completion right down to handing over the keys.

With this information, you will have an idea of the per-square-foot costs to build a house on a certain model using the same materials. You will also have an idea of the size home you can afford to build in that particular style. For example, if the model home is 2,000 square feet and the builder tells you that the turnkey cost to build this house is about $60 per square foot, you simply multiply $60 by 2,000 to get $120,000. Add the typical lot cost to that figure, and you have a good idea what that package of land and building will cost to complete.

Visit several developments with new homes of various styles to obtain a varied sampling of styles and prices. Armed with this information, contact several off-site builders (or, if you're not budget conscious, several custom-home builders). An *off-site* builder is one who purchases *scattered* building lots, which are either leftover lots in older developments or lots acquired independently from individual property owners. A builder who offers an upscale price is usually a *custom-home builder.* The scattered-lot builder is usually a small independent builder who builds a limited number of homes each year and normally stays with several house designs that have proven successful.

Show the builders what you have in mind. Tell them what you have to spend (less about 10 percent of what you can actually afford), and see what prices they come up with. Subtly pick their brains for names of suppliers and subcontractors. Find out what they know about lot costs and construction costs. Ask about the engineers and surveyors they use. Let them know indirectly that you are considering building the home yourself. Their egos will probably not let them believe that you will succeed, and they will try their hardest to scare you into securing their services. Don't. You can do it yourself, using the same techniques and labor the builders do.

Subtly pick their brains for names of suppliers and subcontractors.

WHAT SIZE AND STYLE HOME DO I NEED?

Have the builders price the size home you want from the basic box (least expensive) structure, and then add the features you want in: vaulted ceilings and skylights or ceramic countertops and sunken bathtubs. This information will give you a menu to choose from in calculating your budget. If you can afford to add those features, great. If not, add what you can.

Remember to keep it simple. If you find that a certain style of home is too expensive, think about designing one of the same size in a less expensive style. Recall Figure 3.1, where the roofline was changed from a simple low-profile line to a higher profile. See where you can save money by eliminating some of the fancy rooflines and possibly several windows or exterior doors. These items are expensive and can be added later. If you are on a tight budget, simply frame out the wall area where you would like more doors and windows as if you were going to install them now, and plan to install them some time in the future when you have the money. When you figure that installing a 36-inch-by-48-inch window costs an estimated $300 including material, you can save hundreds and even thousands by postponing that installation. However, your window will be much easier to install at a later date if the framing is already installed in the wall from the beginning.

Often, a young family just starting out with the first home (starter home) can afford only the basic box-style low-profile home with the basic amenities. If the young people couldn't afford a rear deck but would like one in the future, we would install a sliding glass door and install a block of wood in the track to stop the door from sliding open accidentally. Later, when they had the money, they would add the deck and remove the wooden block.

Find a good architect with a reputation for designing good homes. The scattered-lot builder will most likely have the least expensive architect's name. The local building inspector's office is also a good source for names of local architects. If your intended style is a popular one, the architect probably has several completed plans to choose from. If you are designing in a more contemporary style, the architect will work with you, from the original sketch to the completed plans.

The architect will also be able to help with the surveyor and may also recommend several contractors to

Remember to keep it simple. If you find that a certain style of home is too expensive, think about designing one of the same size in a less expensive style.

use. Once you have a list of all materials to be incorporated into the home, the architect should also be able to give you a fair estimate of what it will cost to build. Her estimate will cover only the hard costs, or brick-and-mortar costs, not the soft costs. *Hard costs* are the actual material and labor expenses to build the home, including all machine time and delivery costs if any—generally any cost attributed to the actual construction. *Soft costs* are the engineer's fee, the surveyor's fee, the attorney's fee, your insurance premiums, and all bank fees including interest charges. Refer to Table 9.4 on page 161 where a sample construction cost schedule is provided that shows how to keep a record of hard and soft costs.

Many home builders do not incorporate the soft costs into their estimates when they figure construction costs. These soft costs add up to thousands of dollars, and you must include them in your estimates. Make sure any quotes given to you by contractors include any charges or costs beyond the costs for material or labor. If there is a delivery charge, a storage fee, or whatever, include it. This way you will have a clear picture of the price of the completed project, and you will not be surprised at the end of the job.

It's Cheaper to Go Up than Out

Remember this statement: *It is less expensive to go up than it is to go out!* The *fixed-cost* areas of construction are usually the most expensive. No matter how large or what style the home is, the cost for *site work* will probably not change much. Site work includes all excavation and grading work for the sewer/septic lines, water/well lines, and foundation and generally all machine time needed to make the site into a livable area.

You will build either a concrete slab or a basement as your foundation and frame the house up from there. You will have fixed costs for a kitchen, bathrooms, a garage, and heating and cooling systems. These are the most expensive single items in the home. The balance of the home will be wood framing, insulation, carpet, paint, and trim—the least expensive items (unless you spend a fortune on custom doors and windows).

Many home builders do not incorporate the soft costs into their estimates when they figure construction costs. These soft costs add up to thousands of dollars, and you must include them in your estimates.

The fixed-cost areas of construction are usually the most expensive.

WHAT SIZE AND STYLE HOME DO I NEED?

This is why a single-story home generally costs more to build per square foot than a two-story home. With a single story, you spend more for site work and concrete for the slab or basement. A two-story home gives you a smaller foundation, which requires less material, labor, and site work to build. You are raising the roof two floors instead of one floor and making it smaller. You then simply fill in the empty space with framing, carpet, and trim.

Let's look at an example: For a single-story home with 2,000 square feet of living space, the foundation would have to be 25 feet wide by 80 feet long. For a two-story home with the same square footage, we need only 1,000 square feet of foundation because we will have two floors of 1,000 square feet each. The foundation now only has to be 25 feet wide by 40 feet long, or half the size at half the cost.

This cost saving is one reason the raised-ranch or split-foyer style (see Figure 3.2) is popular in the eastern states. With this style, you simply take a small ranch-style home, raise it up, and fill in the bottom with framing. About one-third of the lower area becomes the garage, and the balance becomes living space, for a fraction of the cost of an attached garage.

You can also build a simple two-story colonial-style home with an inexpensive standard roofline, as shown in Figure 3.3. You have a low-profile, straight roofline, and the house is rectangular with straight lines. All of the materials are precut to fit this house style with a minimum of waste. The labor costs should be very low because the job takes less time to complete. Later you can add a garage and/or a breezeway or a separate family room on the other side to balance things out.

If you want something more stylish, you can take these basic floor plans and embellish them. Figure 3.4 shows a typical two-story colonial home with a contemporary or postmodern flair. The box has been extended at the living-room end, the porch has been added, and the garage roof has been styled with a dormer at the front.

Remember, every time you add a jig or a jog or make a door larger or add a window, it will cost you money. Start out with a simple floor plan and style. Find

Remember, every time you add a jig or a jog or make a door larger or add a window, it will cost you money.

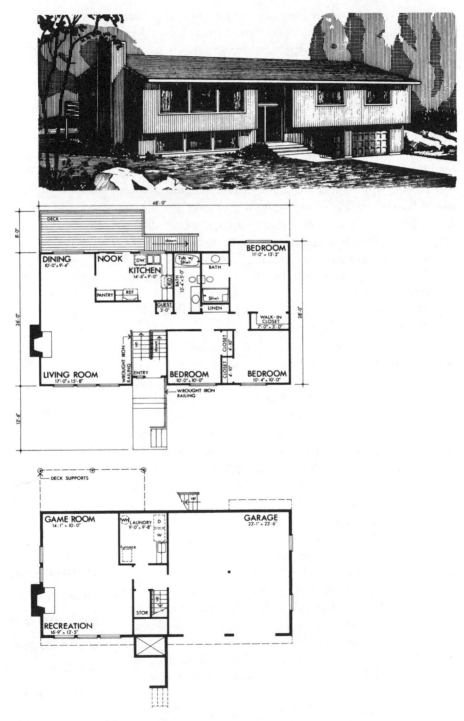

FIGURE 3.2   Raised-ranch or split-foyer style

WHAT SIZE AND STYLE HOME DO I NEED?

UPPER FLOOR

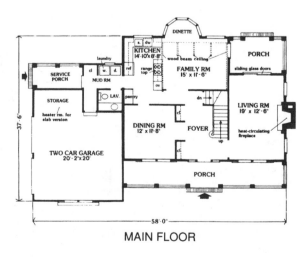

MAIN FLOOR

FIGURE 3.3 Typical two-story colonial style

SAVE $50,000 ON YOUR NEW HOME

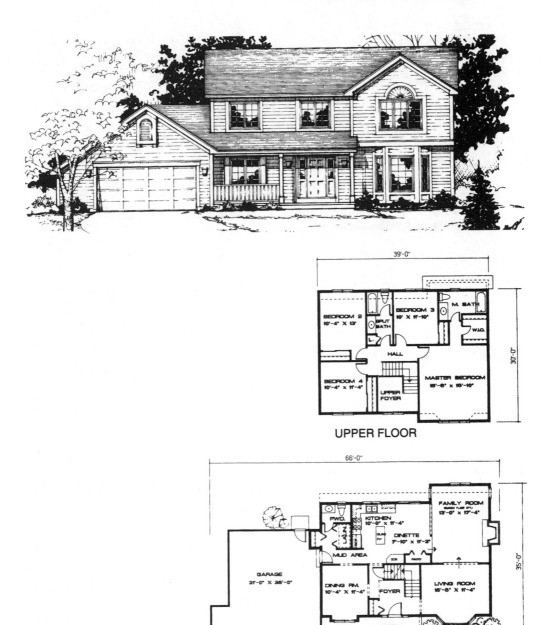

FIGURE 3.4 Two-story postmodern colonial style

the lot that meets your needs, and make sure the package is affordable. If you have money left over, add a few of your wants and have fun.

Living Space versus Square Footage

Although each home you look at has a certain advertised square footage, you do not have that much area to use as living space. Builders measure the *overall square footage,* which means they measure the home using exterior dimensions called *outside to outside.* Your *living space* will be on the inside of the home and will be less than the advertised size.

Interior walls will take up about 100 to 200 square feet of interior space. Add to that figure the hallways, stairways, and closets, and your *actual living space* will be several hundred square feet smaller, even though the builder counts those areas as living space.

To understand how much living space you need, measure the rooms where you now live. Estimate the sizes of the rooms you will need in the new home. Be conservative; you can add later if you find that you can afford to. Lay out the sizes of the bedrooms, bathrooms, dining room, family room, kitchen, and so on. Measure these areas, and total the square footage to see what size home you can be comfortable with. If you have the estimated construction costs from the contractors or the engineer, you will have an idea of what a home of that size will cost (not counting the lot price), assuming conventional materials are used.

Pay close attention to the insulation requirements for your target area. If the winters are cold, you will want to factor in more insulation and better-insulating doors and windows. You might have to forego that rear deck in favor of more energy-efficient items in the house.

Builders measure the overall square footage, which means they measure the home using exterior dimensions called outside to outside.

Home Styles

Here are a few more home styles. Look these over; then go to a bookstore and buy the magazines that show hun-

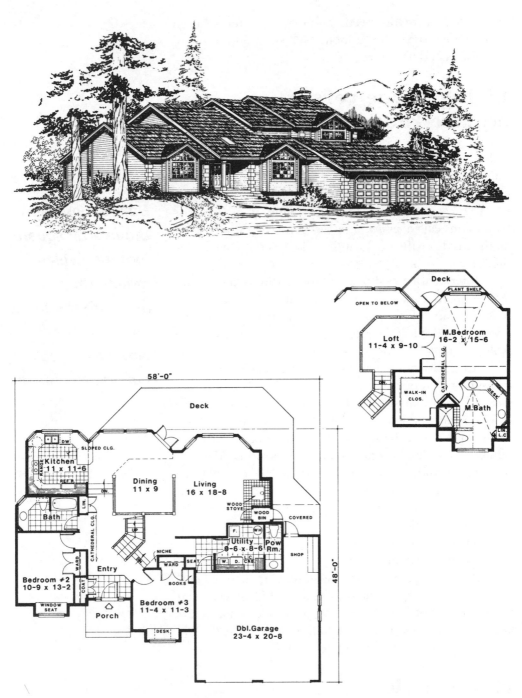

FIGURE 3.5 Contemporary style

dreds of home styles. Find the style that you prefer, but remember to (KISS) keep it simple. Figure 3.5 illustrates the contemporary or modern look. The contemporary style is always a very personal style. What you see as beautiful the next person may consider ugly. The standard ranch-style home, shown in Figure 3.6, has been popular since the 1600s. In the Southwest, you will find the typical Mediterranean-style home, depicted in Figure 3.7, with a masonry tile roof and either one or two stories. Single-story homes are becoming more popular, with the large numbers of retirees moving to desert communities. These homes usually boast vaulted 20-foot ceilings, garden tubs in the master bathrooms, glass-block

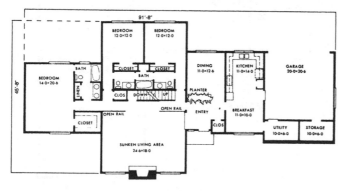

MAIN FLOOR

FIGURE 3.6 Traditional straight ranch style

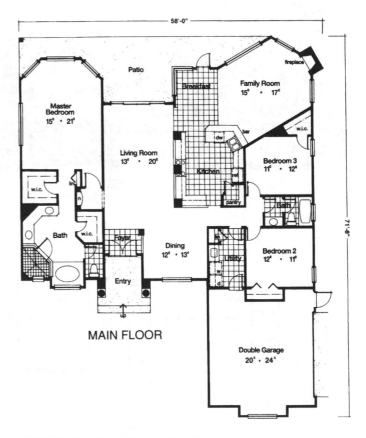

MAIN FLOOR

FIGURE 3.7 Southwestern-Mediterranean style

WHAT SIZE AND STYLE HOME DO I NEED?

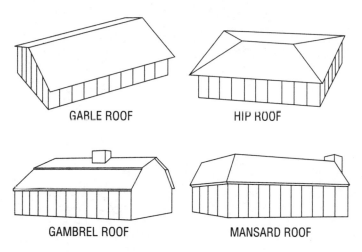

FIGURE 3.8 Rooflines

walls, and much more. They are beautiful and obviously more expensive to build than straight ranch homes. No matter what size home you prefer, the rooflines will set the style. Figure 3.8 shows the various styles of rooflines.

Remember, you should begin with a home in a simple, inexpensive style. Make sure you have the living space you need. If your budget allows you to spend more on the style of the home, be careful—the costs can add up very fast—and have fun!

Remember, you should begin with a home in a simple, inexpensive style. Make sure you have the living space you need.

CHAPTER
4

Finding the Right Building Lot

Buyer's Agent/Seller's Agent

The simplest way to find the largest number of available building lots is to contact a real-estate agent *who specializes in land.* I emphasize this because I have found that a *minority* of licensed agents sell land and approved building lots.

When you contact a real-estate agent, don't assume that he automatically knows everything about all phases of the industry. Real estate is one of the largest industries in the world, and expertise in any area requires years of study. Ask the agent if he is qualified to help you find your dream location. If he balks at that question, ask to be introduced to an agent who has experience in land sales. Inquire whether the agent has allegiance to any developer. Is he the developer's exclusive agent? If so, he owes his allegiance to the seller, not to you. The same holds true if the agent has a favorite developer or development. If he has an established relationship with a seller, question whether the agent can represent your interests over and above that relationship.

Certain real-estate offices also have provisions stipulating that if the agency represents a seller of numerous land parcels, the brokers will ask the agents to channel their land buyers to that client. This arrangement is good

The simplest way to find the largest number of available building lots is to contact a real-estate agent who specializes in land.

Many of these agents will belong to the National Association of Realtors® (NAR), an association that holds its members to a much higher standard than those of state licensing boards.

If your level of affordability is $100,000 and the turnkey price for the house is estimated at $75,000, it is easy to see that you can afford to spend $25,000 for the building lot— right? Not true!

for the seller, but you may miss a good buying opportunity simply because you were not advised that other properties were available.

In certain areas of the country, primarily in the East, it is customary to be represented by one agent throughout the entire transaction. In certain states, that is the law, and *that agent must represent the seller* at all times. In most realty transactions in these areas, you are left to negotiate on your own; you will need to be represented by an attorney (see Chapter 2).

In other regions, primarily in the West, there are two distinct groups of licensed agents with separate responsibilities. A *seller's agent* represents only the seller, and a *buyer's agent* represents only the buyer. If you call an agency and make an appointment with the buyer's agent to see property, the agent must disclose to you that he or she is your (the buyer's) representative. If you find a property that is listed with another agent, the *listing agent* will be representing the seller as the seller's agent. Your agent will make the offer and help you negotiate the transaction; the seller's agent will do the same for the seller.

Many of these agents will belong to the National Association of Realtors® (NAR), an association that holds its members to a much higher standard than those of state licensing boards. In my experience, sales agents who adhere to the educational and ethics requirements of the NAR handle their business in a very professional manner.

Where Do I Look?

Sit down with the real-estate agent and outline your needs and wants. You have an idea of what you can afford to spend for the entire package; you have an idea of what your house will cost. That leaves you with an idea of what you can afford to spend for the building lot.

If your level of affordability is $100,000 and the turnkey price for the house is estimated at $75,000, it is easy to see that you can afford to spend $25,000 for the building lot—right? Not true! You will also incur expenses in buying the lot. There will be fees for the engineer to verify that the lot is suitable for the type of home you want. There will be transfer taxes, and there may be title charges and legal fees. Find out from the agent what closing costs the buyer of a building lot usually pays in your target area. Tell the agent what you can afford to spend, taking into account your costs to buy the lot, *less a little extra.* You want some negotiating room. For example, if your lot budget is $25,000 and your costs to buy the lot are $2,000, you will have $23,000 remaining. If something else comes up—a permit fee or subsurface rock removal or whatever—you will need a small cushion. Say that you have $18,000 to spend for a building lot, and let the agent find one that meets your needs.

You will want your engineer to verify that the lot is buildable. You will need the surveyor to verify the lot lines and the size of the lot. If the property has recently been surveyed by another surveyor, consider using that surveyor to save time and money as the work has already been done. One professional will not certify the work of another. Once you know what your expenses will be, you have an idea where to look.

Location, Location, Location

Location, location, location: If nothing else that I have heard in this industry is true, these three words are definitely true. Drive through several developments, and try to spot what you would consider the best location for a home. Write down the reasons why you think that location is best. Do the same for the worst location, and write those reasons down.

Now take out a local map and find the schools, the medical facilities, the closest interstate access, the railroad station, the airport, the shopping malls, and the local recreation areas. You want to avoid areas of heavy industrial activity because of noise and pollution. You want to avoid any high-crime areas. Also avoid areas exposed to heavy air traffic or road noise. You are probably starting to target the nicest areas of town, but you may find that your budget will not allow you to purchase in these areas.

You are just beginning your search, and there is more than one approach. Try to concentrate your search in areas that will offer you some convenience in daily life.

Try to concentrate your search in areas that will offer you some convenience in daily life.

53

How Do I Find the Lot?

The real-estate agent can help you focus your search. The agent should be able to access the multiple listing service (MLS) via computer or listing book to find out if any lots are available in your target areas. The agent may have in-house listings or may simply know other agents who have listings.

Carry a local map with you. When you find an area you like, mark it on the map. When you find lots that you like, mark the streets where those lots are located. When you get home, you will have an overview of the entire area and the locations of your chosen lots within that area.

If an agent is not successful in finding the right lot for you, you will have to strike out on your own. There are three ways to find the property yourself. One is to drive up and down the streets in your target area to find "for sale by owner" signs. If you find a lot this way, make sure your purchase is *subject to your engineer's approval,* and hire an attorney or an experienced, licensed agent to represent you in the sale. Ask the engineer to give you an idea of the cost of site improvements *before* you talk price with the seller.

If you don't have any luck with this approach, you may have to dig deeper and use a search technique that I have found very effective. As you drive around, you may see parcels of vacant land sandwiched between homes. These vacant areas, known as *off-site lots,* may be owned by each adjoining neighbor for privacy, they may have been set aside in the development for utilities, or they may be owned by absentee owners who bought intending to build and never did. If you find a vacant parcel that you like, write down the names of the owners on both sides of the lot. Go to the tax assessor's office, and ask for the vacant-lot owner's name and address. This is public information.

Contact the owner and ask if he or she is willing to sell. You will usually find that the owner has never listed the property for sale, has lived outside the area for some time, and is not familiar with local property values. This is good. If you can convince the owner to sell, you may

Carry a local map with you. When you find an area you like, mark it on the map.

also convince him or her to sell with terms. We will discuss how to buy the lot in the next chapter.

The third way to find a lot is to locate several developments where vacant lots are for sale directly from the developer. Here you will find fully engineered and surveyed lots, known as *on-site lots,* ready to build on (but have them checked out anyway). In most subdivisions, the most desirable lots—high, good-drainage lots or lots with a view—sell first and for the most money. The sales continue until the least desirable and least expensive lots remain. If only a few lots are left, be careful. What appears to be a cheap lot is probably just that. The lot appears okay until you look into the costs of improving it to make it buildable. Usually, by the time you have finished filling the hole or cutting the rock or draining the water, you could have purchased a much better lot without all the problems.

On-site lots may cost more than older, off-site lots. When the off-site lot was developed, the property values probably were much lower, and the improvement requirements were less stringent. The on-site lot will be new, and the cost of land and improvements will also be higher. As a trade-off, on-site lots will also reflect higher market values for new homes. Homes in the off-site area will be older and consequently less valuable than the new homes.

Make sure that any agreement you enter into to buy a lot specifies your right to have your engineer verify that it is buildable and within your budget.

What Is a Good Lot?

If your target area is in the East, a wooded lot would be your preference. In the desert, something with a mountain view would be nice. However, although these attributes add value, they do not make the lot a good, buildable lot.

Water! Rock! Fill! These are the words in construction that send shivers up any builder's spine. Any of them must be dealt with, and it will cost money. Water must be allowed to drain away. Rock must be removed. A low area must be filled with extra material, which must be purchased.

What appears to be a cheap lot is probably just that.

Water! Rock! Fill! These are the words in construction that send shivers up any builder's spine.

You should try to find a building lot with an elevation that will allow water to drain away from the proposed house location. The house should be located on the highest portion (if the lot is large enough) of the lot. Figure 4.1 is a simple illustration of good lot elevation. The house is located higher than the road and the surrounding area. Any water from heavy rainfall will drain away from the house, and if the area is landscaped, you shouldn't experience erosion.

The house is located higher than the road and the surrounding area.

Before purchasing any building lot, I have included in my contract a requirement that I have the right to inspect for water or rock by digging holes all over the lot to a depth of about 14 feet. But, on two lots I remember in New York State, I still came up short. In one case, my partner and I accepted an engineer's study that showed a particular lot to be all good, drainable (permeable) gravel soil. The location was good, the price was right, and the neighborhood was fine, so we bought it. We held that lot until the following spring to catch the spring housing market. We started digging and had the foundation (a full 11-foot foundation) completed when we had a period of rain. Because we had bought a gravel lot, we were not worried—until several days later, when we went to the job and found water covering the footings and creeping up the foundation walls.

We could not understand what the problem was until we looked into the distance, about a mile or so in every direction, and realized that our lot rested at the bottom of a geographical low point. Figure 4.2 illustrates how the *surface water* will obey gravity and drain to the lowest point. With our lot, all of the water in the surrounding area was draining down to the lowest point and raising the *water table*. Figure 4.3 shows the difference

WATER DRAINS DOWN AND AWAY
FROM THE PROPOSED HOUSE LOCATION

ROAD

　　　　FIGURE 4.1　Good lot elevation

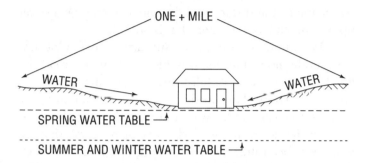

FIGURE 4.2 Water drainage/water tables

between surface water and *groundwater* and the rising of the water table.

You have to study the surrounding area for as much as several miles in all directions to see if the lot sits at a low point and will be subject to flooding or washing out in heavy rain. My partner and I realized later that the engineer had tested that lot in the summer when it was dry and found no evidence of a high water table. The moral of the story? Test the lot yourself, and double-check the surrounding elevations.

Rock accounts for another potential major expense and may even make the lot unbuildable. *Surface rock* is obvious, and you can see evidence of it as you walk the lot. The danger is *subsurface rock*, or rock that you cannot

GROUND SURFACE ACCUMULATES SURFACE WATER FROM RAIN

WATER FILTERS DOWN TO THE CAPILLARY LAYER
WHERE GROUNDWATER AND SURFACE WATER MEET

WATER TABLE RISES

EXISTING WATER TABLE FROM GROUNDWATER →

FIGURE 4.3 Rising water table

The danger is subsurface rock, or rock that you cannot see.

see. Some of the surface rock in evidence may be a small tip of a much larger section that is buried.

We found an example of subsurface rock a lot in a new subdivision. The lot was higher than the road for good drainage. It was fully engineered and ready for building permits. The existing trees were small, and our expense to clear the lot was minimal. We dug about 20 holes in that lot trying to find water or rock. All that we found was beautiful, rich, *permeable* (good, drainable) soil. The house was to be a 3,600-square-foot postmodern contemporary that would sell for $360,000. The plans called for a large full basement with 11-foot ceilings. We started excavation for the foundation, which would be sunk into the ground to a depth of 8 or 9 feet, and we hit rock at the rear corner of the foundation. Why hadn't we found the rock when we tested? Figure 4.4 shows how rock can hide below the surface and why you never know where you will find it.

You can see why you can't be too careful when you investigate a building lot. In the western states it is customary to build slab-on-grade (concrete slab on grade level) instead of using a full or partial foundation. I will explain more about construction techniques in later chapters.

The third item of concern in lot acquisition is the cost of *fill*, or material that you must bring in to meet construction requirements or local building codes. Fill can be anything including simple dirt to fill a low area, rock to fill a swampy area, or more expensive graded material for the

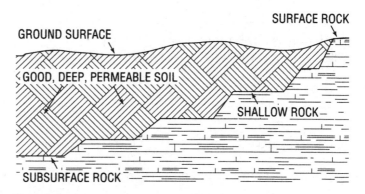

FIGURE 4.4 Surface and subsurface rock

lot or septic system. I recently met with a local builder in Nevada who thought he had found a bargain. He had bought two lots in an older section of town for $30,000 each. (The going rate for a lot in this area is about $40,000. Remember what I said about leftover lots in a development.) The builder was delighted to have found this bargain until he discovered that local building codes required the top of the lot at ground level to be at least 1 foot above the street level. Unfortunately, the lots he had bought were 6 inches *below* street level. He had to purchase enough fill to bring the lots to the required 12 inches above the street and pay for the machine time to spread and compact the fill. By the time he was finished, those lots cost him an additional $15,000 per lot, or $5,000 more than the going rate for good lots in the same area.

If a particular building lot is selling for less than the current price of similar lots in the same area, ask yourself why. In my experience, no one gives anything away, and if something is cheap, I want to know what's wrong with it.

The lot elevations are also known as the *topography* of the lot. Figure 4.5 shows a side view of the topography of a property. A topographical map, which, if available, you can obtain from an engineer or surveyor, will show you the high and low points. You can often determine the lot elevations better by looking at a topographical map than by walking the property. With this information you can gauge which areas might need to be filled and where to locate the house to allow drainage away from the foundation.

Figure 4.5 shows the high and low areas of the lot. You can see that the elevations are taken at 5-foot intervals. (Your local codes may require 2-foot intervals.) You can also see that the lot is higher than the road and that it is 5 feet higher in the back than in the front. The topographical view shows that the lot is relatively flat and that

Fill can be anything including simple dirt to fill a low area, rock to fill a swampy area, or more expensive graded material for the lot or septic system.

If a particular building lot is selling for less than the current price of similar lots in the same area, ask yourself why.

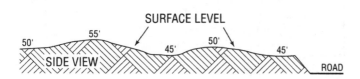

FIGURE 4.5 Side-view topographical elevations

you must be careful to build the house high enough to allow for drainage. If the lot is small and you cannot find enough fill material on site to allow a higher foundation, you may have to bring in additional fill. If the lot is large enough, you may be able to cut down the front and rear areas, push that material toward the center of the lot, and provide a higher area for the foundation. This sounds easy, but it will cost additional site-work money for machine time and perhaps material as well.

Buyers always say they want a flat lot. I say, Good luck! I'll take a lot with an elevation any day: When it rains, my lot will drain.

Buyers always say they want a flat lot. I say, Good luck! I'll take a lot with an elevation any day: When it rains, my lot will drain. Ask yourself, When it rains, where will all that water go? If the lot is flat and the ground becomes saturated, the water will find the path of least resistance and drain into your home!

Figure 4.6 shows a top view of a topography. If any topographical map exists for your area, this is most likely the view you will see. Here, as in the side view, the elevation lines are at 5-foot intervals, and the lot is relatively flat toward the back but is 15 feet higher in the front. The elevation lines are much closer at the front of the lot; this indicates a steep incline with a sharp 10-foot drop as you move from front to back on the lot. The topographical map lets you see all of this information about the lot without setting foot on it. When you do walk the lot, you will have a much better understanding of the property.

Because you know that the steep area is the location of the road access, you know you will have to spend additional money to cut that area down to allow access into the lot. The cut-down material may be spread over other

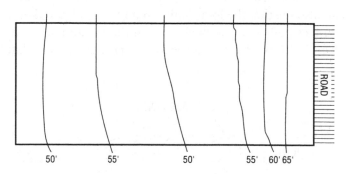

50'   55'   50'   55' 60' 65'

FIGURE 4.6   Top-view topographical elevations

areas of the lot. Watch for rock in this area. If you see rock along the roadsides where the road has been cut, you will probably find rock on this lot as well. Make sure that your contract allows testing for rock, fill, or water. Make sure that your contract allows you to cancel the agreement and get your money back if improvement costs exceed a certain amount.

Lots with water or sewer or paved road frontage in place will cost more than those without such improvements.

Lots with water or sewer or paved road frontage in place will cost more than those without such improvements.

Walking the Lot

Topographical maps and surveys can give you a good idea of the elevations and dimensions of the building lot, but there is nothing like physically walking the property to get a real feel for it. Ask the owner for a copy of the survey. If one is not available, ask the tax assessor's office for a copy of the tax map that includes your target parcel. Figure 4.7 shows what lot numbers from a tax map might look like. The tax map designation for this example would be "Map No# 6158, Block 02, Lot Number 230031." This would make the legal description from the tax map 6158-02-230031.

The measurements on the tax map will not be as accurate as the actual survey, but they will be close enough. Locate the scale on the tax map or the survey so you can estimate distances by using a ruler. For example, if the scale is 1″ = 100′, then 1 inch equals 100 feet, 2

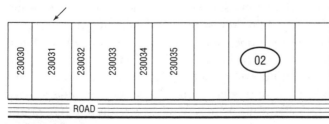

MAP NO# 6158

FIGURE 4.7   Tax map lot number

inches equal 200 feet, and so on. A measurement of 150 feet would be $1^1/_2$ inches on the map.

Every property has characteristics that make it unique among properties.

Every property has characteristics that make it unique among properties. Walk the frontage of the lot first to get a feel for the distance. A slightly stretched stride will reach approximately 3 feet for a person who is 5 feet, 10 inches tall. If you pace off 100 feet, you should take about $33^1/_3$ paces. If your lot is heavily wooded, it helps to be able to approximate the distances by counting the number of paces it takes to reach a boundary.

Start down the right-hand boundary, walk slowly, and remember to count your paces. Study the interior of the lot as you walk. If there are trees, note what kinds they are and how tall. Are they healthy? Look for small animal burrows or bird nests. If you see an animal burrow, check out the soil around it. This animal may have burrowed down several feet, and the soil deposited around the entry hole is the type of soil you will find in that area. If your lot is open and without vegetation, it is easier to learn what it has to offer. In the eastern states, patches of moss may point to a deposit of clay or underlying rock formation where water does not drain off. Mark those areas with something you will remember, like large rocks. Continue along the right boundary until you come to the end of the property. You should find a surveyor's corner-marker stake or a metal pin in the ground that marks the corner of the lot. If there is no evidence of a corner marker, you should be near the corner if you have continued to pace off the distance indicated on the plot plan or map.

Continue your walk along the rear boundary, and try to watch the elevations through the interior of the lot as you walk. Is the lot higher or lower from front to back? Is it higher on the right side or the left side? Remember, water will drain to the lowest point. Make sure your proposed house location does not sit at the lowest area of the lot. If it does, change the house location or buy another lot.

Remember, water will drain to the lowest point.

Continue your walk to the other rear corner, turn the corner, and follow this (left-hand) boundary back toward the front. All the while, study the interior of the lot and the properties that adjoin your lot. Verify that the surrounding properties will not cause a problem of drainage onto your property that you will have to deal with. Check your plot plan for notes of any trees, stone walls, or fences that may be helpful in locating the lot lines. Look into the distance if you can, and see how the surrounding terrain affects your land. If the surrounding land is higher than your property, verify that water draining from the surrounding areas will not cause you a problem. Also, recall Figure 4.2, which depicts seasonal differences in the water table due to rain or snowfall.

Be wary of a lot that appears to have been filled in. A filled lot is acceptable if *clean fill* was used and if the fill material has been on the lot for at least one year. If the fill contains tree trunks, building material, large rocks, or chunks of concrete, be careful. You will have to dig through this material to install your utilities and foundation, and the costs may be prohibitive. Also, if you plan to install a well for drinking water, it is crucial to avoid contaminated fill. All things break down over time, and certain materials release toxic chemicals that leach into the surrounding soil. You don't want those chemicals seeping into your well water. If the lot has been filled with biodegradable material, such as large trees, that matter will rot over time, and the soil will sink into the areas where it was deposited. *Have the seller or developer sign an affidavit that the lot you are considering has not been filled or that if fill was used, only clean fill was used.*

I have seen new subdivisions where the developer cut rock in one section and used it to raise the lots in the lowest part of another section, covering the rock with a thick layer of soil to hide what had been done. The developer made more money on the raised lots, but the builders or owners had to spend more money drilling and cutting through the rock to build the homes. Also, recently filled lots, even those filled with rock, must be allowed time to settle before being built on. If fill is not allowed to settle, the weight of a new home will eventually cause the loose rocks and soil to compact, and the house will experience severe damage due to later settling.

In the desert Southwest, the main problem is erosion. Because there is little natural vegetation to absorb and hold water, when it rains in the mountains, the water accumulates first into rivulets. As the water continues downhill, it accumulates more runoff and grows into streams. The volume continues to increase until it may

Have the seller or developer sign an affidavit that the lot you are considering has not been filled or that if fill was used, only clean fill was used.

If your target lot is near a wash or what appears to be a dry streambed, be careful.

reach flash-flood proportions. If your target lot is near a *wash* or what appears to be a dry streambed, be careful. A wash is an indication that water has traveled down through an area with enough force to carve into the soil a ditch, where any water will flow to when it rains. You don't want to be living next to this area if and when a flash flood decides to take that particular wash down the hill.

If a wash or drainage ditch is evident, ask the building inspector and possibly the town or county engineer what the history has been and what the risks are for that particular area.

If you see evidence of rock, either visible surface rock or moss-covered areas where rock make be, note these areas, and make your purchase subject to verification that the rock will not be a problem for what you want to build. I will cover more details about buying the lot in the next chapter.

The Sleeper Lot

If you are looking at off-site lots in older subdivisions and you find a spot that appears to be a larger-than-average lot for that area, you may have found a parcel where someone combined several lots to form a larger lot for privacy or investment and never built on it. Find out who owns it and whether it is for sale. Before you try to negotiate with the owner, check with the tax assessor's office to see whether that parcel has one number or more than one number assigned to it for tax purposes. If more than one lot number has been assigned, you may have the opportunity to buy a parcel comprising several lots for not much more than the cost of an average building lot. I call such lots "sleepers." If the owner thinks the parcel is only one lot, you may get a bargain, but verify with the zoning officer and building inspector that each lot meets the requirements to build.

See if you can find where the parcel was divided into more than one lot.

If there is one assigned lot number, ask to see the original subdivision maps for the development. Ask to see the older assessment maps. See if you can find where the parcel was divided into more than one lot. Ask whether the lot was resubdivided or the lot lines were moved to make it larger or the assessor simply assigned one number to more than one lot. If the latter is true, the lots may remain legally subdivided, and you still may be able to purchase several lots at a good price. I have purchased several properties this way and ended up with two lots for a little more than the current price of a single lot. Verify the answers to all of these questions with the local zoning and building inspection officials.

Is the Lot Approved for Building?

When you are looking at property, ask the owner if the lot has any current approvals for building. Has anyone applied for permits to build? Has any engineering been done for well/water or septic/sewer approval? How old are the approvals? If the lot is part of an older subdivision and there are no recent approvals, check with the local building inspector for the current requirements to build on that lot.

Building codes and permit requirements change constantly, and you need to know whether a lot meets current permit requirements without your spending money to make improvements before permits can be issued. If improvements are required, such as extending the water line or blacktopping the road, and if the seller wants top dollar, he or she will have to make the lot buildable for you. If the seller is unwilling to do so, negotiate the cost of the improvements less a little extra for your risk. If that is not agreeable, find another lot.

If the lot is in a newer subdivision or has approvals to build, the owner should have a current *plot plan, drawn and stamped by a licensed engineer* and showing the lot lines, the lot elevations, the proposed house location, the proposed water/well and sewer/septic locations, and the driveway. The plan should also show any large trees, fences, stone walls, and outbuildings that may exist. It should also indicate the boundaries of the adjoining lots. Figure 4.8 shows a typical plot plan. You can see that the location for the house is a flat area and that the property drops down from front to back to allow for drainage. The

Building codes and permit requirements change constantly, and you need to know whether a lot meets current permit requirements without your spending money to make improvements before permits can be issued.

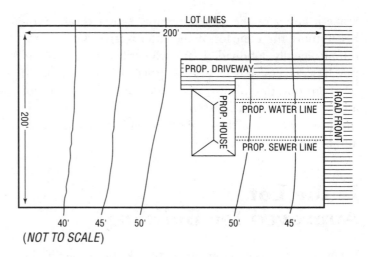

(*NOT TO SCALE*)

FIGURE 4.8 Plot plan with topographical overlay

200-foot-by-200-foot lot multiplies out to a 40,000-square-foot lot. A lot this size is considered a builder's short acre; an acre is actually 43,560 square feet.

One major item to look for on an approved plot plan or an approved subdivision map is the engineer's notes.

One major item to look for on an approved plot plan or an approved subdivision map is the *engineer's notes*. They may be anywhere on the page. These notes detail what improvements are or will be required in order for construction to be allowed on a particular lot. If there are problems within the subdivision, such as drainage or rock, you should see somewhere on the plan the engineer's indication that certain areas must be filled or excavated. You will see what types of water or sewer services must be installed. The engineer will list the numbers of lots where improvements are required or will indicate somewhere on the subdivision map where extra work must be done to make a particular lot buildable.

This engineer works for the developer or the seller. If problems exist, the seller does not want to show them on the map. However, the engineer must show them to comply with licensure laws. To placate the seller, the engineer may bury the notes in small type in peripheral areas on the page or may even place them on a separate page. If the engineer's notes are not evident on the subdivision map, ask to see those notes before you make a decision. If the lot requires additional work to make it buildable, make the purchase subject to your engineer's review, and inform the seller that you want him or her to make the lot buildable before you buy.

If the lot has no approvals at all and you must start from scratch to get the lot approved—for instance, if the owner is out of state—make sure you buy the lot for less (much less if you can) than the going rate for approved lots in the area. After all, you are taking the risk to get the lot approved. Make your contract with the seller subject to your engineer's and surveyor's testing the lot to see if it is buildable and subject to the issuance of all required permits. You certainly do not want to buy the lot if (although you gain the approvals) the town passes a moratorium against all building permits and you can't build on it anyway.

Tell the seller that you don't want to tie up a large down payment because you are paying for all of the approvals. Offer several hundred dollars as a down payment instead of several thousand, with the down payment refundable in full in the event you cannot gain the approvals. In that case, all engineering is to be turned over to the seller as compensation for having the property off the market, and your money is to be refunded. I will cover the lot purchase more extensively later in this chapter.

I have done this type of purchasing many times with great success. Most often, I bought the lots for rock-bottom prices compared to the prices of surrounding parcels.

You certainly do not want to buy the lot if (although you gain the approvals) the town passes a moratorium against all building permits and you can't build on it anyway.

The Beacon Hills Syndrome

I'll tell you about a situation that may lead you to affordable building lots where others might fear to tread. I call it the Beacon Hills Syndrome, for an area where I found the most remarkable bargains.

Beacon Hills is an area in New York's Duchess County that was originally planned and developed in the late 1950s as a summer colony to be sold to the New York City market, about an hour and a half away by car or train. The lots were considered small, 25 feet wide by 100 feet deep, in an area of acre-plus developments.

When I entered the building business in the 1970s, there were areas in the county that were preferred by upscale buyers for custom homes. There were plenty of building lots for average middle-income buyers. However, there were few areas for first-time buyers or for those who could not afford or did not want to spend the amounts necessary to enter the middle or upscale home markets.

Being new to the home-building business and not having deep pockets, I needed to get the most for my money. I also wanted to begin my new business in a market that had plenty of buyers and not much competition—and that was the first-time-buyer or lower-priced-home market.

Because Beacon Hills was originally a summer colony, with a number of summer cabins in the development, the property values were lower than in other developments in other areas of town. The school district that served Beacon Hills also has its own problems, which contributed to the negative aura surrounding the area. Unbelievably, the local real-estate agents warned customers away from this area (because they did not have any listings there), and the area was labeled a problem area.

I had found an area that my competition didn't want and that had prices I could afford.

I thought it was wonderful. I had found an area that my competition didn't want and that had prices I could afford. One problem was locating the owners of the many vacant lots, which I did by using the assessor's office to obtain names and addresses. The second problem was that because the area had since been rezoned to require larger building lots and none of the lots conformed to the existing zoning ordinance, they were considered *nonconforming lots*. (I'll explain zoning in the following section.) The third problem was that, in many cases, the lot owner had died *intestate*—without leaving will to transfer his or her interests to the heirs—and the title was in question.

So the area had its problems. What the heck, I could afford it. If you are on a tight budget and can't find a building lot that you can afford to buy, check your target area for situations like Beacon Hills. They may be in older areas, but if they appear acceptable, give it a try.

The first thing to do is locate the current lot owners. Ask each one if he or she is the original owner (that is, the first buyer after the lot was subdivided by the developer). If so, you're in luck: This person will have the original deed and will have paid the least money for the lot. If not, ask if the owner has clear title to the land. If the original owner has died, did he or she will the property to the current owner? Did the owner acquire the property at a tax sale, and if so, does he or she have total or partial title to the lot? Satisfy the question of *clear title* in advance. If the title is not clear, find out what must be done to make it clear. You may have to file an *action to quiet title* if there are questions of who owns what. Consult with your attorney regarding matters of title.

If the title is clear, you may still have to buy more than one lot to satisfy the zoning requirements. Check with the zoning official to verify the amount of land required to meet current zoning needs. Considering the number of lots you need, you can now formulate an offer.

Because I had little competition in the Beacon Hills, I didn't offer much for the lots. Most of the owners had owned their lots for many years, paying taxes all that time, and thought the lots were worth much more than they were actually worth. I went to the assessor's office and obtained documentation on the most recent sales in the area. Fortunately, the sale prices were far less than for the other (more desirable) developments. I convinced the owners that those figures represented all the land was worth, and many said they would rather sell than continue holding the land.

I offered each lot owner a few hundred dollars as a down payment, subject to issuance of a building permit and financing from my lender to build a house. I also offered the owners terms that were more for my benefit than for theirs. I offered them my 10–40–50 deal: 10 percent of the purchase price on contract, an additional 40 percent to be paid when the house was under roof and I closed on my construction loan, and the balance of 50 percent when I closed the house to a buyer or in six months, whichever came first.

This approach allowed me to buy lots for little money down and to finance the balance using the banks' and the owners' money. It also gave me the opportunity to tie up more property and build more houses than I otherwise could have. I paid interest to all the sellers, and everyone came out a winner.

Satisfy the question of clear title in advance.

I offered each lot owner a few hundred dollars as a down payment, subject to issuance of a building permit and financing from my lender to build a house.

Most municipalities have established zoning laws that designate particular areas for commercial, industrial, and residential uses.

Don't be afraid to seek out other areas that meet your financial needs. If you run into a roadblock, find a way to get around it if at all possible. Make it work!

What Is Zoning?

When an area grows to the point where one neighbor begins to *encroach on* another's property—for instance, the chicken farmer wants to increase the flock from 10 chickens to 1,000 and that change will have an impact on your property—it is time to establish zoning.

Most municipalities have established zoning laws that designate particular areas for commercial, industrial,

FIGURE 4.9 Zoning map

TABLE 4.1 Permitted Uses in a Zoning Ordinance

Dist.	Permitted uses	Accessory uses	Lot size	Lot width	Lot depth	Front yard	Rear yard	One side	Both sides	Min. floor area	Max. lot coverage	Bldg. height
R-40	Residential	Churches	40,000	150'	150'	50'	40'	25'	50'	1,000'	25%	35'
R-20	Residential	Twin, buildings	20,000	100'	125'	40'	40'	15'	30'	900'	25%	35'
R-10	Residential	Veg. stand	10,000'	75'	100'	35'	40'	12'	24'	800'	20%	30'
C-1	Commercial	Bowling	55,000'	150'	200'	75'	40'	35'	70'	2,000'	35%	30'

and residential uses. Depending on the available utilities and the terrain of the area, the zoning ordinance will designate the lot sizes, the setback requirements, the sizes of the homes to be built, the numbers of stories to be built, and much more. Figure 4.9 shows an example of a zoning map. You can see the various area designations, such as R-40 for 40,000-square-foot lots and C-2 for an area designated for commercial use. You can also see areas along the main roads designated for town center use and further commercial use. The outlying areas in the R-120 zone will allow building lots up to 120,000 square feet or 3 short acres.

Typically there will be a zoning map or official who can tell you what your target area is zoned for. Buy a copy of the zoning ordinance, find the lot size designation that pertains to your lot, and read the restrictions. You should see a portion of the ordinance that sets forth the *principal permitted uses*. These are uses for the property that do not require any further approval by the town or city zoning or planning board. Table 4.1 is an example of a "use" directory in a zoning ordinance.

If you encounter a lot that is sandwiched between two existing homes and the area has been rezoned, it may qualify as a *grandfathered* lot. This means that the lot existed before the implementation of the zoning ordinance and therefore cannot be required to adhere to the existing zoning requirements. If the ordinance recognizes grandfathered property, you may be allowed to build on such a lot under the old requirements.

Another way to solve the old-versus-new zoning problem is to apply to the local *zoning board of appeals*. This board has the power to grant a *variance* from the

Typically there will be a zoning map or official who can tell you what your target area is zoned for.

zoning law if a property cannot meet the requirements and a *hardship* is created for the owner. Make your purchase subject to the granting of the variance; have the seller apply for the variance because he or she is the taxpayer for the property.

Don't be afraid to explore possibilities and try new things.

Don't be afraid to explore possibilities and try new things. When my partner and I were building a home in Beacon Hills, I wanted to play with the backhoe. I'd never taken the time to learn to use heavy equipment, and I wanted to try my hand at moving some dirt. I climbed into the machine, raised the front bucket, raised the rear bucket, put it into gear and, went nowhere! I looked at my partner, who was laughing so hard that he was purple in the face. I realized my mistake: I had forgotten to raise the hydraulic stabilizers on each side of the machine, and all I accomplished was to make those big wheels spin in the air. We all had a good laugh, but at least I wasn't afraid to try.

Board of Health Approved (B.O.H.A)

When you ask whether the lot is approved, find out what it is approved for. In the East, B.O.H.A. stands for Board of Health Approved. This means that a county health department engineer was present at the soil testing to approve the drainage and the well and septic location. The same official also approved the design and installation of septic systems. Septic systems are explained later in this book. Different areas have different requirements, but the bottom line is the same: If you are to pay market value, you want the lot approved and ready to build without spending more money for engineering, surveying, soil testing, drainage, clear title, water, sewer, soil removal, or municipal fees. If any of these items will cost more money, you will pay less for the land to compensate.

Have your engineer review the approvals for each lot.

Have your engineer review the approvals for each lot. With enough money you can get almost any lot approved, but you may not want to pay the cost of implementing the necessary approvals. If the approvals require excessive work, question the validity of the purchase.

FINDING THE RIGHT BUILDING LOT

Why put more money into the ground than is necessary? Buy a better lot, and put your money into the house.

Be careful of fees charged by the municipality. Make sure you are familiar with fees that will be charged by the town or county for the issuance of building permits. These fees can be excessive, and they are not advertised by anyone. The building inspection department will have a schedule of permit fees; consult this schedule before you agree to a lot purchase price. In larger cities, the lot fees may have increased to $20,000 per lot.

A building lot is considered *improved* if the road frontage is a paved road. The extent of existing lot improvements is important. Many lenders will not lend money against a totally unimproved lot. Another category of improvement would be the availability of existing water, sewer, gas, or power lines.

If your lot lies within a newer subdivision, the improvements should already be installed; all you have to do is connect to the existing systems. Check with the building inspector's office regarding fees you must pay to connect to the central water and sewer systems. Also, ask whether you can hire your own contractor or whether the municipality has its own contractor do the work for a fee. The utility company should provide at least 100 feet of cable to the home without charge unless you are required to bury the utilities. If the utilities are underground, there is usually a charge for the work.

Also ask how detailed the plot plan must be, how many copies must be supplied, and to whom they must be given. In a rural area, a simple sketch drawn to scale may be sufficient. In an urban area, you may be required to have your engineer draw the plot plan with a topographical overlay showing all projected improvements. The municipality may require a before-and-after overlay to show how the lot will look after the work is done. It may require a separate plan for each phase of construction, including electrical and plumbing drawings for the house.

You can see why the approval process may be expensive. It pays to verify everything with the municipality before you enter into a purchase agreement to buy the lot.

Check with the building inspector's office regarding fees you must pay to connect to the central water and sewer systems.

73

CHAPTER
5

Acquiring the Building Lot

Control the Building Lot

You've figured the cost of construction for the size home you want to build. You've qualified for the financing. You've selected the style you want. You've done your homework and are aware of the costs for the financing and the required approvals. You've searched and found that perfect building lot, and now it's time to sign on the dotted line.

Nervous? Don't be. You are taking a big step, but remember—thousands of people are building homes every year, and there is no reason for you to stop now. This chapter will tell you how to maintain control of the property with very little risk.

You need time to do your final investigation regarding the condition of the lot. You may want to have the soil tested or the survey done. You certainly want your engineer to have access to the lot in order to lay out the plot plan. You want to make sure you receive a written commitment for the financing, and the lender cannot give one without knowing which lot you are buying and what the price is. You also need time to locate subcontractors and obtain final bids from them to complete the package cost. I will cover subcontractors in the following chapters. This chapter shows you how to get the building lot off the market to gain the time you need.

This chapter will tell you how to maintain control of the property with very little risk.

The Art of the Deal

The purchase offer agreement to buy a building lot alone is similar to the one used in buying a resale home. It could even be the same form. Study the sample contract in Figure 5.1.

Once you have done all the homework and have satisfied yourself that the lot will accommodate your needs, you need to make your offer contingent upon all the information you were given. If the lot is offered as an approved building lot, make the offer contingent upon your acceptance of all approvals. If the lot is offered as improved, again, make the offer contingent upon verification and acceptance of all improvements.

If the lot is offered as an approved building lot, make the offer contingent upon your acceptance of all approvals.

If you plan to build on the lot in the near future, make the offer contingent upon review and approval of the lot information by your excavation and foundation contractors. These contractors will not be able to give you final job prices until they have seen the lot. They will need to examine the information and provide you with a list of costs for required improvements beyond the cost of the house. Therefore, another contingency is your acceptance of the final prices offered by your contractors. If you have consulted with an engineer, include your acceptance of your engineer's report as an additional contingency. If you are applying for financing as part of a package deal with a lender or just as part of the purchase price, that's another contingency.

You also want the purchase contingent upon the seller's providing clear and marketable title to avoid any unknown problems.

You also want the purchase *contingent upon the seller's providing clear and marketable title* to avoid any unknown problems. It would be a good idea to engage a title company to do a *title search* to make sure there are no hidden problems. *I am not an attorney, and I cannot offer legal advice. I advise you to contact an attorney to receive help with the contract, the title, and the proper deed.* See an example of a typical bargain and sale deed in Figure 5.2.

Another form of deed is the *quit claim deed.* Be careful of this form of title. A quit claim deed does just that: It allows the owner to transfer title simply by quitting any claim to ownership he or she may have to the title. This form of deed is used quite often in a divorce situation, where one spouse quit claims to the other.

ACQUIRING THE BUILDING LOT

CONTRACT FOR SALE
(for a vacant lot)

Seller and Purchaser agree as follows:

Seller's Name:

Seller's Address:

Purchaser's Name:

Purchaser's Address:

1. Seller shall sell and Purchaser shall buy the Property on the terms stated in this contract.
2. The Property is described as follows:

    (Include a legal description of the property.)

Note. In the event that the Seller is unable to convey to the Purchaser a clear and marketable title to the premises as described above, in accordance with this contract, prior to the closing date, the sole obligation of the Seller will be to refund to the Purchaser the amount paid on account of the purchase price, and upon such refund, this contract shall be considered canceled.

(a) All right, title, and interest the Seller may have lying on any street or highway to the center lines thereof.
(b) Makes reference to any articles of personal property used in connection with the property. If you do not offer to buy that old tractor that sat upon the land for 50 years, there is no personal property included in this sale.

3. The sale includes: (a) All buildings and improvements on the property.

    (Include any other items included in the sale.)

4. The purchase price is:

    $ _____
    payable as follows:

On the signing of this Contract, by check subject to collection:

    $ _____

By assuming any existing mortgages of:

    $ _____

By Purchase Money Note and Mortgage from Purchaser to Seller:

    $ _____

Balance in cash or certified check on delivery of the deed:

    $ _____

FIGURE 5.1   Sample land contract   *continues*

The BALANCE DUE AT CLOSING is payable by bank or certified check.

5. Refers to any existing mortgages that have to be satisfied.
6. Refers to any Purchase Money Mortgages that the Seller agrees to hold.
7. Sets forth any contingencies such as:
   (a) Building and zoning regulation.
   (b) Conditions, agreements, restrictions, and easements of record.
   (c) Any statement of facts an inspection or survey of the property may show if it does not make the title unmarketable.
   (d) Any existing tenancies.
   (e) Any unpaid assessments payable after transfer of title.

This is where you would either enter your list of contingencies or make reference to an attached addendum that sets forth your requirements.

8. Specifies the type of deed to delivered to the Purchaser.
9. Lists the adjustments expected at closing, such as taxes.
10. Lists any adjustments for water or sewer meter readings (there shouldn't be any for vacant land).
11. Specifies that this agreement does not provide for what happens in the event of fire.
12. Designates the time and place for closing—remember, "on or about" a certain date, not "on or before." You will have contingencies that must be satisfied; give yourself plenty of time.
13. Makes reference to a broker's fee as the Seller's responsibility.
14. Specifies that all moneys paid on behalf of the property shall become liens thereon but that the liens shall not continue after the Purchaser defaults.
15. States that this agreement cannot be changed orally.
16. Makes the agreement binding upon the distributees, executors, administrators, successors, and assigns of both parties.

FIGURE 5.1   *continued*

Execution of a quit claim does not mean that you will receive clear and marketable title. There may be all sorts of problems with the property, and by accepting the quit claim you may just inherit those problems.

The title search will show any liens filed against the property and any easements that may be present. An *easement* may be an area where a public utility has a power line running over a portion of the lot or a water, sewer, or drainage pipe running underground. See Figure 5.3 for examples of easements.

ACQUIRING THE BUILDING LOT

BARGAIN AND SALE DEED

CONSULT YOUR LAWYER BEFORE SIGNING THIS INSTRUMENT—
THIS INSTRUMENT USED BY LAWYERS ONLY

THIS INDENTURE, made the _____ day of _____,
nineteen hundred and

BETWEEN

_____
(Seller's name and address)

party of the first part, and

_____
(Purchaser's name and address)
party of the second part,

WITNESSETH, that the party of the first part, in consideration of Ten
Dollars or other valuable consideration paid by the party of the second
part, does hereby grant and release unto the party of the second part,
their heirs or successors and assigns of the party of the second part
forever,

ALL that certain plot, piece or parcel of land with the buildings and
improvements thereon erected, situate, lying and being in the (Town
of Anywhere, State of Anywhere) and further described as (beginning
at a stake at the corner of a property owned by whomever and
wherever road, thence so many feet so many degrees so many
minutes south to a stake, thence so many feet so many degrees so
many minutes west to a stake, thence north so many feet, degrees
and minutes, thence east so many feet, degrees and minutes to the
point of the beginning). Being further described as: (Insert tax grid
number and street address.)

TOGETHER with all right, title, and interest, if any, of the party of the
first part in and to any street and road abutting the above described
premises to the center lines thereof; **TOGETHER** with the
appurtenances and all the estate and rights of the party of the first
part in and to said premises; **TO HAVE AND TO HOLD** the premises
herein granted unto the party of the second part, the heirs or
successors and assigns of the party of the second part forever.

AND the party of the first part covenants that the party of the first part
has not done or suffered anything whereby the said premises has
been encumbered in any way whatever, except as aforesaid.

AND the party of the first part, in compliance with Section-13 of the
Lien Law, covenants that the party of the first part will receive this
consideration for this conveyance and will hold the right to receive
this consideration as a trust fund to be applied first for the purpose of

FIGURE 5.2   Typical bargain and sale deed   *continues*

paying the cost of the improvement and will apply the same first to the payment of the cost of the improvement before using part of the total for any other purpose. The word "party" shall be construed as if it read "parties" whenever the sense of this indenture so requires. **IN WITNESS WHEREOF,** the party of the first part has duly executed this deed the day and year first above written:

In Presence of:

FIGURE 5.2 *continued*

> *A lien could be any type of debt left unpaid by a contractor, a debt owed to a bank, or even unpaid taxes.*

There are many forms of easements; your attorney will help you understand them. A *lien* could be any type of debt left unpaid by a contractor, a debt owed to a bank, or even unpaid taxes. You don't want to get everything ready to go and find out the seller never paid his taxes. Buy a title insurance policy to protect your interest in the title.

Find out what type of deed the seller is offering. Make sure you receive a *trust deed,* a *bargain and sale deed with covenants against grantor's acts* (Figure 5.2), or a *full covenant and warranty deed.* These deeds offer you protection in the event the seller knowingly deceives you. For example, imagine a scenario in which the seller says that the lot was purchased from a woman after the death of her husband. She maintained that the lot had been willed to her and that she had the right to sell it. In reality, however, the husband had died intestate, and other members

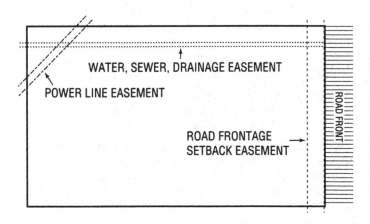

FIGURE 5.3 Examples of easements

of his family may have a claim against the property. With the right form of deed, you will have legal recourse to hold the seller responsible, or the title company will have to pay if it didn't uncover the mistake.

If the lot requires the performance of soil tests or other approvals, include those as contingencies as well. *If you plan to build in the near future, make your offer contingent upon the issuance of a building permit for the house you wish to build to make sure that you can actually build on the lot and there is no moratorium in effect.* Even if you plan to build months or years later, if possible, have the building permit issued anyway to ensure that the lot will be grandfathered if the zoning changes.

Most building permits are issued with a requirement that the structure be completed within 6 to 12 months. A permit can be extended if the municipality approves the extension. You can have a permit issued even if the original plans you submit for approval differ from the plans you actually follow, as long as they are similar. In most areas, you can resubmit another set of building plans for the same permit and pay a small fee to have the building inspector approve the second set of plans.

Make the purchase offer contingent upon the drafting and signing of a formal contract of sale within a specified time. This puts pressure on the seller to either accept or reject the offer, and you will know where you stand that much sooner.

If the purchase offer is drawn up by a real-estate broker and is considered a binding contract and you are represented by an attorney, make the agreement also contingent upon your attorney's review and approval. If the lot you want is part of a new subdivision, that subdivision must have been filed with the county clerk's office and issued an identifying file number. You should be able to obtain a copy of the *filed map* from the county so you can review all the engineer's notes and pertinent information concerning the subdivision and the ways it may affect your lot.

Another protection is to make the purchase contingent upon the accuracy of all the information filed under the subdivision's name, together with the filed-map number and the date the map was filed. If you have a problem in the future and it can be proven that the seller or the

Make the purchase offer contingent upon the drafting and signing of a formal contract of sale within a specified time.

83

seller's engineer or surveyor made a mistake, you may have recourse to file for damages against those individuals because your purchase was contingent upon the information provided on the filed map. A last contingency should be your lender's final approval of the entire package.

All of these contingencies may seem cumbersome, but they will protect you if it turns out that the information provided to you was faulty. In that case, you will be able to void the transaction.

All of these contingencies may seem cumbersome, but they will protect you if it turns out that the information provided to you was faulty. In that case, you will be able to void the transaction. Remember—you have control of the property, and you have time to formalize the balance of the agreements you need to make sure your project goes smoothly.

You have negotiated some of the terms by including certain contingencies in your offer, but you also need to negotiate the price and terms for payment. Having satisfied yourself that the lot is worth buying, you need to make an offer to buy it at the best price and on the best terms you can get. If you have done your homework to verify the lot value, you can offer less money than the owner is asking—say about 10 percent to 20 percent less than the asking price—but the terms of the purchase may influence the seller's response. If your offer includes all the contingencies I have mentioned, the seller will want to know how long you will take to satisfy yourself that the contingencies can be met. He or she will not want the lot off the market for a considerable time. You will have to negotiate a time frame agreeable to the seller and move as fast as you can to satisfy the terms you included.

If the purchase is for all cash, that consideration should carry a lot of weight with the seller, and you should find him or her more agreeable to your other terms. If you are offering a down payment and asking the seller to hold a mortgage, the seller may negotiate a little harder on the price and other terms. If you plan to put down a small down payment, say 5 to 10 percent, the seller will probably hold firm on the price. *Money talks, and the more cash paid down, the better the terms should be.*

If you have already been approved for long-term financing and you are short on cash, one way to tie up the lot without actually buying it, using a small down payment, is to offer the seller an *option-to-purchase* agreement instead of an actual sale contract. You agree to pay the seller an amount for the option to buy the property within a certain time. The option fee can be one year's property taxes with the same contingencies as the contract. You can also draft both the option agreement and the contract at the same time, with the option agreement beginning immediately and the contract to take over when you decide to exercise the option to buy the property. This approach allows you to take control of the sale: The property is off the market, and you haven't paid out a lot of money before you are ready.

Another way to negotiate the purchase without a lot of cash—and this requires some risk on the seller's part—is to offer a 10–40–50 deal. You pay the seller 10 percent of the purchase price on the signing of the contract. You are allowed to begin construction of the house without actually owning the lot. (However, if you or your builder structures the financing using a *construction loan*, the lender will require you to be *owner-in-title* when you are ready to close the construction loan and receive your first draw from the lender.)

You have the house built at least to the finished frame, siding, and roof; that means your first draw from the lender when you close the construction loan will be substantial. At the construction loan closing, you pay the seller an additional 40 percent of the land price (using the lender's money), and the seller takes back a second mortgage for the 50 percent balance owed on the lot. The seller will have to subordinate the second mortgage to the lender's first mortgage (the bank or lender is always in first position in the event of a default). Because you are improving the property with a new house and you are allowed to draw only so much as the construction progresses, the seller should feel safe (you hope). Now you have paid 50 percent of the land cost, with only 10 percent paid out of pocket. The remaining 50 percent can be paid as a percentage of each construction draw from the lender or paid in full at the final closing of your permanent mortgage. The trick is to keep the construction schedule ahead of the payments to the contractors and the material vendors to the point that you can use the lender's money to pay for the land.

It sounds tricky, but when you don't have the cash, you have to become inventive to achieve your goals. No

This approach allows you to take control of the sale: The property is off the market, and you haven't paid out a lot of money before you are ready.

It sounds tricky, but when you don't have the cash, you have to become inventive to achieve your goals.

one gets hurt, the seller gets his or her money, the contractors make their profits, the lender gets its interest, and you get your house. The danger in this arrangement is that if you do not pay the subcontractors regularly to keep them happy, they will refuse to work, and the job will slow down or stop. If this happens, you cannot draw more money from the lender because of the lack of work, and the entire project is in jeopardy. *You must make sure to adhere to a work-payment schedule that allows you to draw as much money as possible without losing momentum. If you are not absolutely sure this can be done, don't play games. Find the cash, or buy a less expensive property.*

Some lenders will package the loans into one closing instead of two. This is a distinct advantage because it lets you avoid double closing costs. This type of package allows you to purchase the lot for cash, using the financing. Purchasing all in cash puts you in a better bargaining position, and you might make a better deal for the lot.

Any form of package financing should allow for *interest-only* payments during the land acquisition and construction phases. You will be billed only for interest for the amounts you have used; the interest is charged and repaid to the lender monthly. Certain lenders will allow the interest to accrue, with payment deferred until you're ready to close the permanent loan and move in.

You will have to provide the building inspector with copies of the plot plan, the house blueprints, and the list of materials to be incorporated into the house and pay the permit fee. The bank will want a copy of these materials for the appraiser, who will verify the value. The title company will want a copy of the survey or plot plan to verify the lot dimensions. You will need 10 to 15 copies of each document for the various contractors so they can give you bids for the costs of labor. You will want several copies for the suppliers so they can bid on the costs of materials. You will want several copies to play with as you move through the process. Don't you appreciate all of those general contractors just a little more now?

Make sure you have enough cash available for down payment, mortgage applications, contractor advances, and engineer, surveyor, and attorney fees. Save enough to buy yourself a stiff drink.

Some lenders will package the loans into one closing instead of two. This is a distinct advantage because it lets you avoid double closing costs.

CHAPTER 6

Getting the Show on the Road

Finalize the Package

When you begin working with your engineer to have the blueprints drawn or approved, ask her for at least 10 copies of the *check print*. They cost a fraction of the price of blueprints. You will give these check prints out to the various contractors. Review Figure 6.1 to see the components of a typical house.

If you are not familiar with construction techniques, I highly recommend that you hire a project manager who has general contracting experience and a general contractor's license if the municipality requires one. Certain states require all contractors to be licensed. To obtain a license, a contractor must prove that he or she has the necessary experience. A project manager will charge a fee for his services (a fair fee is 10 percent of the total cost of the job). However, I am not in favor of the percentage fee system; I don't see that it gives the contractor incentive to save money. I prefer a flat-fee payment, with a bonus if the job comes in under budget. For example, if the expected cost of construction (not including the cost of the land) is $100,000, offer the project manager a $10,000 flat fee payable as follows:

- $1,000 in advance

I am not in favor of the percentage fee system; I don't see that it gives the contractor incentive to save money.

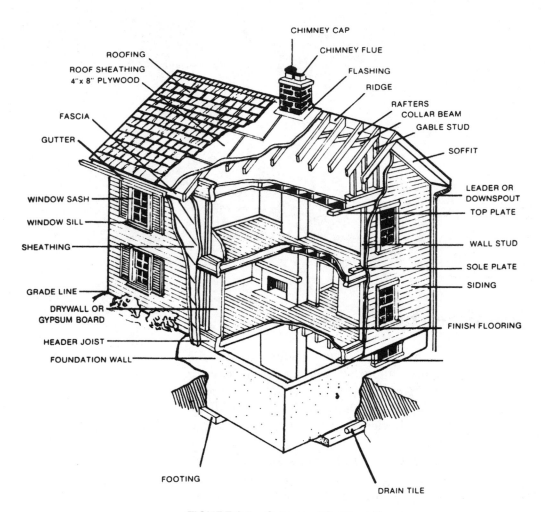

FIGURE 6.1 Cutaway side view of house

- $2,500 when the house is under roof with electric and plumbing roughed in and exterior excavating completed, all contracting bills have been satisfied, and all contractors have submitted payment waivers

- $2,500 when the interior is completed and painted, carpet and tile are installed, exterior siding is completed, all ground work is done, and all contractors have submitted payment waivers

- $2,000 when all appliances have been delivered; all house heating, cooling, electrical, plumbing, and water systems are approved and operational; and all contractors have submitted payment waivers

- $2,000 when the house has been inspected by the building inspector, the certificate of occupancy has been issued by the building inspection department, and you have the keys and verification that all contractors have been paid and waivers submitted

Offer to pay the manager an additional 10 percent of whatever money he can save you.

Meet with the Building Inspector

Go over a set of blueprints and the plot plan with the building inspector. I have found this practice to work in my favor. Most building inspectors are not paid high salaries, yet they are responsible to the municipality to ensure that builders build according to federal and state codes. I know this sounds strange, but there are contractors out there who don't always tell the truth. The inspectors are constantly on the lookout for cheaters, and they may have developed thick skins over the years.

When I was the new boy on the block in each town, I made it my business to meet with the local building inspectors and town engineers to introduce myself and explain what I wanted to accomplish. I asked for their input and guidance. Without fail, I made new friends, my projects were always approved, and the jobs progressed smoothly.

Do the same with the lender's representative. Ask to meet with that person for a few minutes to present a completed blueprint, plot plan, and materials list. Invite the representative to view the site once the roof is on. Offer to buy lunch. Now you have made a friend, and the flow of money should be smooth.

The inspectors are constantly on the lookout for cheaters, and they may have developed thick skins over the years.

Meet with the Engineer

Ask your engineer or your project manager to provide you with a simple construction schedule. You need to know how many days each phase is likely to take.

Armed with this information, you can establish your budgets and estimated time schedules for bank draws, inspections, and material deliveries—and if the seller is holding a mortgage, for that payment schedule as well.

Organize Your Files

Be prepared with your own checklists to make sure the job is moving along according to the budget and the timetable.

Make absolutely sure that you obtain copies of all paid contractor invoices and waivers.

Be prepared with your own checklists to make sure the job is moving along according to the budget and the timetable. As the job progresses, you can keep track of how much money is being spent, where the money is spent, and whether the contractors are performing according to their bidding prices and times. Table 6.1 is an example of a simple construction checklist.

As you progress through the construction process, make absolutely sure that you obtain *copies of all paid contractor invoices and waivers.* You don't want to get to the end of the line just to find out that there was a dispute with a particular contractor and that if he or she is not paid, you cannot close the loan.

The construction process for the average home takes about 90 days to complete. If your home will be a custom or larger-than-average home, add more time. To be safe, if you assume the project will take about 120 days, you won't be disappointed. Why does it take so long? You are one small builder of one house. Contractors make their money working on as many jobs as they can physically handle, and if a builder of multiple homes needs your contractor's services, you will either have to wait or hire another contractor to complete the job. If you have taken my advice and hired a general contractor as a project manager, he will have a rapport with many contractors, and your project should proceed at a much faster pace.

GETTING THE SHOW ON THE ROAD

TABLE 6.1 Construction Checklist

Preconstruction	*$ Bids*	*Dates and $ Completed*
☐ Blueprints		
☐ Materials list		
☐ Project manager agreement		
☐ Survey completed		
☐ Insurance in place		
☐ Permits issued		
☐ Bank fees paid		
☐ Licenses issued/paid		
☐ Performance bonds paid		
☐ Water/sewer tap fees paid		
☐ Other fees paid		

Construction begins		
☐ Clear and grade lot		
☐ Excavate for water and sewer		
☐ Excavate for electrical		
☐ Excavate for footings		
☐ Pour footings		
☐ Install water and sewer		
☐ Pour or install block foundation		
☐ Install rough under plumbing		
☐ Grade exterior lot		
☐ Pour concrete slab		
☐ Frame exterior walls		
☐ Frame interior floors		
☐ Frame interior walls		
☐ Frame roof		
☐ Install roof tiles		
☐ Install rough electric		
☐ Install rough plumbing		
☐ Install rough heat and HVAC		
☐ Install windows and exterior doors		
☐ Install insulation		
☐ Install Sheetrock		
☐ Paint interior		
☐ Paint or stain exterior		
☐ Install kitchen and bath floors		
☐ Complete install plumbing		
☐ Complete heat and HVAC		

TABLE 6.1 *continued*

Construction begins	$ Bids	Dates and $ Completed
☐ Install kitchen and bath cabinets		
☐ Install light fixtures		
☐ Install kitchen and bath sinks		
☐ Paint touch-up		
☐ Final repairs		
☐ Install all appliances		
☐ Obtain all appliance warranties		
☐ Install carpets		
☐ Test all systems		
☐ Order final certified survey		
☐ Obtain certificate of occupancy from building inspector		
☐ Make a final punch list		
☐ Order final closing		

Notes:

_____

_____

_____

_____

_____

_____

_____

_____

_____

_____

_____

Remember that time is money in the construction business.

Remember that time is money in the construction business. A sum of $50,000 borrowed at an annual interest rate of 9 percent interest, comes to $12.33 per day. If you have to wait 10 days for a contractor, the wait gets expensive. If you have to wait for several contractors and your project comes in a month behind schedule, it gets really expensive. As you continue to borrow money, the interest continues to escalate. That concern doesn't even take into account the potential for your mortgage interest to increase. Most banks will hold your approved rate for at least 90 to 120 days; after that, they will adjust for market conditions.

DESCRIPTION OF MATERIALS

☐ Proposed Construction   No. _____
                                                       (To be inserted by FHA or VA)

☐ Under Construction

Property address _____ City _____ State _____

Mortgagor or Sponsor _____   _____
                             (Name)   (Address)

Contractor or Builder_____   _____
                             (Name)   (Address)

INSTRUCTIONS

1. For additional information on how this form is to be submitted, number of copies, etc., see the instructions applicable to the FHA Application for Mortgage Insurance or VA Request for Determination of Reasonable Value, as the case may be.

2. Describe all materials and equipment to be used, whether or not shown on the drawings, by marking an X in each appropriate check-box and entering the information called for in each space. If space is inadequate, enter "See misc." and describe under item 27 or on an attached sheet. THE USE OF PAINT CONTAINING MORE THAN ONE PERCENT LEAD BY WEIGHT IS PROHIBITED.

3. Work not specifically described or shown will not be considered unless required, then the minimum acceptable will be assumed. Work exceeding minimum requirements cannot be considered unless specifically described.

4. Include no alternates, "or equal" phrases, or contradictory items. (Consideration of a request for acceptance of substitute materials or equipment is not thereby precluded.)

5. Include signatures required at the end of this form.

6. The construction shall be completed in compliance with the related drawings and specifications, as amended during processing. The specifications include this Description of Materials and the applicable Minimum Property Standards.

1. EXCAVATION:
Bearing soil, type _____

2. FOUNDATIONS:
Footings: concrete mix _____; strength psi _____   Reinforcing_____
Foundation wall: material _____   Reinforcing_____
Interior foundation wall: material _____   Party foundation wall _____
Columns: material and sizes _____   Piers: material and reinforcing _____
Girders: material and sizes _____   Sills: material_____
Basement entrance areaway _____   Window areaways _____
Waterproofing _____   Footing drains _____
Termite protection _____
Basementless space: ground cover _____; insulation _____;
    foundation vents _____
Special foundations_____
Additional information: _____

3. CHIMNEYS:
Material_____ _____   Prefabricated *(make and size)*_____
Flue lining: material _____ Heater flue size_____
    Fireplace flue size_____

continues

FIGURE 6.2 HUD materials list form

Vents *(material and size)*: gas or oil heater _____; water heater _____

Additional information: _____

4. FIREPLACES:

Type: ☐ solid fuel; ☐ gas-burning; ☐ circulator *(make and size)*_____

Ash dump and clean-out _____

Fireplace: facing _____; lining _____; hearth _____; mantel _____

Additional information: _____

5. EXTERIOR WALLS:

Wood frame: wood grade, and species_____ ☐ Corner bracing.

  Building paper or felt _____

  Sheathing _____; thickness _____; width_____; ☐ solid;

  ☐ spaced _____"o.c.; ☐ diagonal: _____

  Siding _____; grade_____; type_____; size _____;

  exposure_____"; fastening_____

  Shingles _____; grade_____; type_____; size _____;

  exposure_____"; fastening_____

  Stucco_____; thickness_____";

  Lath _____; weight_____lbs.

  Masonry veneer _____ Sills _____ Lintels _____ Base flashing _____

Masonry: ☐ solid ☐ faced ☐ stuccoed; total wall thickness_____";

  facing thickness_____"; facing material _____

  Backup material _____; thickness_____"; bonding _____

  Door sills _____ Window sills _____ Lintels _____ Base flashing _____

  Interior surfaces: dampproofing, _____ coats of _____; furring _____

Additional information: _____

Exterior painting: material _____; number of coats_____

Gable wall construction: ☐ same as main walls; ☐ other construction _____

6. FLOOR FRAMING:

Joists: wood, grade, and species _____; other _____;

  bridging _____; anchors _____

Concrete slab: ☐ basement floor; ☐ first floor; ☐ ground supported;

  ☐ self-supporting; mix _____; thickness _____";

  reinforcing_____; insulation_____; membrane_____

Fill under slab: material _____; thickness _____".

Additional information: _____

7. SUBFLOORING: *(Describe underflooring for special floors under item 21.)*

Material: grade and species _____; size _____; type_____

Laid: ☐ first floor; ☐ second floor; ☐ attic _____ sq. ft.; ☐ diagonal; ☐ right angles.

Additional information: _____

8. FINISH FLOORING: *(Wood only. Describe other finish flooring under item 21.)*

Location	Rooms	Grade	Species	Thickness	Width	Bldg. Paper	Finish
First floor							
Second floor							
Attic floor_____ sq. ft.							
Additional information:							

9. PARTITION FRAMING:

Studs: wood, grade, and species_____ size and spacing_____

  Other _____

Additional information: _____

10. CEILING FRAMING:

Joists: wood, grade, and species _____

  Other _____ Bridging_____

Additional information: _____

FIGURE 6.2 *continued*

11. **ROOF FRAMING:**
Rafters: wood, grade, and species _____
    Roof trusses (see detail): grade and species _____
Additional information: _____

12. **ROOFING:**
Sheathing: wood, grade and species _____ ☐ solid; ☐ spaced _____ "o.c.
Roofing _____ ; grade _____ ; size _____ ; type _____
Underlay __ _____ ; weight or thickness_____ ;
    size _____ ; fastening _____
Built-up roofing _____ ; number of plies _____ ;
    surfacing material _____
Flashing: material _____ ; gage or weight _____ ;
    ☐ gravel stops; ☐ snow guards
Additional information: _____

13. **GUTTERS AND DOWNSPOUTS:**
Gutters: material _____ ; gage or weight _____ ; size _____ ; shape _____
Downspouts: material _____ ; gage or weight _____ ;
    size _____ ; shape _____ ; number _____
Downspouts connected to: ☐ Storm sewer; ☐ sanitary sewer; ☐ dry-well.
    ☐ Splash blocks: material and size _____
Additional information: _____

14. **LATH AND PLASTER:**
Lath ☐ walls, ☐ ceilings: material _____ ; weight or thickness_____
    Plaster: coats ___ ; finish _____
Dry-wall ☐ walls, ☐ ceilings: material _____ ; thickness _____ ;
    finish_____
Joint treatment _____

15. **DECORATING:** *(Paint, wallpaper, etc.)*

Rooms	Wall Finish Material and Application	Ceiling Finish Material and Application
Kitchen		
Bath		
Other		

Additional information: _____

16. **INTERIOR DOORS AND TRIM:**
Doors: type _____ ; material _____ ; thickness _____
Door trim: type_____ ; material_____ ;
    Base: type _____ ; material _____ ; size _____
Finish: doors _____ ; trim _____
Other trim *(item, type and location)* _____
Additional information: _____

17. **WINDOWS:**
Windows: type_____ ; make_____ ;
    material _____ ; sash thickness _____
Glass: grade _____ ; ☐ sash weights;
    ☐ balances, type _____ ; head flashing_____
Trim: type _____ ; material _____
    Paint _____ ; number coats _____
Weatherstripping: type _____ ; material _____ ;
    Storm sash, number_____

continues

Screens: □ full; □ half: type_____; number_____;
    screen cloth material _____
Basement windows: type _____; material _____;
    screens, number_____; Storm sash, number_____
Special windows _____
Additional information: _____

18. ENTRANCES AND EXTERIOR DETAIL:
Main entrance door: material _____; width_____
    thickness_____".
Frame: material _____; thickness_____"
Other entrance doors: material _____; width_____
    thickness_____".
Frame: material _____; thickness_____"
Head flashing _____ Weatherstripping: type _____; saddles_____
Screen doors: thickness_____"; number _____
    screen cloth material _____
    Storm doors: thickness _____"; number _____
Combination storm and screen doors: thickness_____"; number_____;
    screen cloth material _____
Shutters: □ hinged; □ fixed. Railings _____, Attic louvers _____
Exterior millwork: grade and species _____
    Paint _____; number coats_____
Additional information: _____

19. CABINETS AND INTERIOR DETAIL:
Kitchen cabinets, wall units: material _____;
    lineal feet of shelves _____; shelf width_____
    Base units: material _____; counter top _____; edging _____
    Back and end splash _____ Finish of cabinets _____; number coats_____
Medicine cabinets: make _____; model _____
Other cabinets and built-in furniture _____
Additional information: _____

20. STAIRS:

Stair	Treads		Risers		Strings		Handrail		Balusters	
	Material	Thickness	Material	Thickness	Material	Size	Material	Size	Material	Size
Basement										
Main										
Attic										

Disappearing: make and model number _____
Additional information: _____

21. SPECIAL FLOORS AND WAINSCOT   Wainscot   Floors

Location	Material, Color, Border, Sizes, Gage, Etc.	Threshold Material	Wall Base Material	Underfloor Material
Kitchen				
Bath				

Location	Material, Color, Border, Cap, Sizes, Gage, Etc.	Height	Height Over Tub	Height in Showers (From Floor)
Bath				

FIGURE 6.2 *continued*

Bathroom accessories: ☐ Recessed; material _____; number _____;
☐ Attached; material _____; number _____.
Additional material: _____
22. PLUMBING:

Fixture	Number	Location	Make	Mfr's Fixture Identification No.	Size	Color
Sink						
Lavatory						
Water closet						
Bathtub						
Shower over tub △						
Stall shower △						
Laundry trays						

△ Curtain rod   △ Door   ☐ Shower pan: material _____
Water supply: ☐ public; ☐ community system; ☐ individual (private) system. *
Sewage disposal: ☐ public; ☐ community system; ☐ individual (private) system. *
*Show and describe individual system in complete detail in separate drawings and specifications according to requirements.
House drain (inside): ☐ cast iron; ☐ tile; ☐ other _____
House sewer (outside): ☐ cast iron; ☐ tile; ☐ other _____
Water piping: ☐ galvanized steel; ☐ copper tubing;
☐ other _____ Sill cocks, number _____
Domestic water heater: type _____;
make and model _____; heating capacity _____ gph. 100° rise.
Storage tank: material _____; capacity _____ gallons.
Gas service: ☐ utility company; ☐ liq. pet. gas; ☐ other _____
Gas piping: ☐ cooking; ☐ house heating.
Footing drains connected to: ☐ storm sewer; ☐ sanitary sewer; ☐ dry well.
Sump pump; make and model _____
capacity _____; discharges into _____
23. HEATING:
☐ Hot water. ☐ Steam. ☐ Vapor. ☐ One-pipe system. ☐ Two-pipe system.
☐ Radiators. ☐ Convectors. ☐ Baseboard radiation.
Make and model _____
Radiant panel: ☐ floor; ☐ wall; ☐ ceiling. Panel coil: material _____

☐ Circulator. ☐ Return pump. Make and model _____
_____; capacity _____ gpm.
Boiler: make and model _____
Output _____ Btuh; net rating _____ Btuh.
Additional information: _____
Warm air: ☐ Gravity. ☐ Forced. Type of system _____

Duct material: supply _____; return _____
Insulation _____, thickness _____ ☐ Outside air intake.
Furnace: make and model _____
Input _____ Btuh.; Output _____ Btuh.

continues

Additional information: _____

☐ Space heater; ☐ floor furnace; ☐ wall heater. Input _____ Btuh.;

Output _____ Btuh.; number units _____

Make, model _____

Additional information: _____

Controls: make and types _____

Additional information: _____

Fuel: ☐ Coal; ☐ oil; ☐ gas; ☐ liq. pet. gas; ☐ electric;

☐ other _____; storage capacity_____

Additional information: _____

Firing equipment furnished separately: ☐ Gas burner, conversion type.

☐ Stoker: hopper feed ☐; bin feed

Oil burner: ☐ pressure atomizing; ☐ vaporizing_____

Make and model_____ Control_____

Additional information: _____

Electric heating system: type _____

Input _____ watts; @ _____ volts; Output _____ Btuh.

Additional information: _____

Ventilating equipment: attic fan, make and model _____;

capacity _____ cfm.

kitchen exhaust fan, make and model _____

Other heating, ventilating, or cooling equipment _____

24. ELECTRIC WIRING:

Service: ☐ overhead; ☐ underground. Panel: ☐ fuse box; ☐ circuit-breaker;

Make _____ AMP's_____ No. circuits_____

Wiring: ☐ conduit; ☐ armored cable; ☐ nonmetallic cable; ☐ knob and tube;

☐ Other _____

Special outlets: ☐ range; ☐ water heater; ☐ Other _____

☐ Doorbell.   ☐ Chimes.   ☐ Push-button locations _____

Additional information: _____

25. LIGHTING FIXTURES:

Total number of fixtures _____

Total allowance for fixtures, typical installation, $_____

Nontypical installation _____

Additional information: _____

26. INSULATION:

Location	Thickness	Material, Type, and Method of Installation	Vapor Barrier
Roof			
Ceiling			
Wall			
Floor			

HARDWARE: *(make, material, and finish.)* _____

SPECIAL EQUIPMENT: *(State material or make, model and quantity. Include only equipment and appliances which are acceptable by local law, custom and*

FIGURE 6.2 *continued*

applicable FHA standards. Do not include items which, by established custom, are supplied by occupant and removed when he vacates premises or chattles prohibited by law from becoming realty.) _____

_____
_____
_____
_____
_____
_____
_____
_____

27. **MISCELLANEOUS:** *(Describe any main dwelling materials, equipment, or construction items not shown elsewhere; or use to provide additional information where the space provided was inadequate. Always reference by item number to correspond to numbering used on this form.)* _____

_____
_____
_____
_____
_____
_____
_____
_____
_____
_____

PORCHES:

_____
_____
_____

TERRACES:

_____
_____
_____

GARAGES:

_____
_____
_____

WALKS AND DRIVEWAYS:
Driveway: width_____; base material_____"; thickness_____"
    surfacing material_____; thickness _____"
Front walk: width_____; material _____; thickness_____".
Service walk: width_____; material _____; thickness_____".
Steps: material _____; treads_____"; risers_____".
Cheek walls_____
OTHER ONSITE IMPROVEMENTS:
(Specify all exterior onsite improvements not described elsewhere, including items such as unusual grading, drainage structures, retaining walls, fence, railings, and accessory structures.)

_____
_____
_____

LANDSCAPING, PLANTING, AND FINISH GRADING:

Topsoil _____ " thick: ☐ front yard; ☐ side yards;

☐ rear yard to _____ feet behind main building.

Lawns *(seeded, sodded, or sprigged)*: ☐ front yard _; ☐ side yards _; ☐ rear yard _

Planting: ☐ as specified and shown on drawings; ☐ as follows:

_____ Shade trees, deciduous, _____ " caliper.

_____ Low flowering trees, deciduous, _____ ' to _____ '

_____ High-growing shrubs, deciduous, _____ ' to _____ '

_____ Medium-growing shrubs, deciduous, _____ ' to _____ '

_____ Low-growing shrubs, deciduous, _____ ' to _____ '

_____ Evergreen trees, _____ ' to _____ ', B & B.

_____ Evergreen shrubs, _____ ' to _____ ', B & B.

_____ Vines, 2-year _____

_____

_____

Identification. — This exhibit shall be identified by the signature of the builder, or sponsor, and/or the proposed mortgagor if the latter is known at the time of application.

Date _____ Signature _____

Signature _____

FHA Form 2005
VA Form 26-1852

FIGURE 6.2 *continued*

After the engineer provides you with the required sets of blueprints, you need to fill out and submit a materials list (spec sheet) to the bank, the building inspector and all the contractors to show them what materials will be incorporated into the house. Figure 6.2 is an example of a common materials list provided by the U.S. Department of Housing and Urban Development (HUD).

CHAPTER
7

Matching Good Contractors with Good Prices

Find Good Contractors

As I urged in the preceding chapter, if you have no knowledge or experience in construction, do yourself a favor and hire an experienced general contractor for the entire project. Pay that person a flat fee (10 percent of the cost of the job is not unusual) with bonuses or as the job progresses, and enjoy the experience. If you can't find a general contractor who can satisfy your needs, try to convince one of the contractors you wish to hire to oversee the project and advise you along the way. Try to find one contractor who has a long history in the area and the industry. He or she will probably know most of the contractors in the area and be able to help you find the good ones. Offer that key person extra payment for advice, and you should make an extremely valuable friend.

Inform all contractors that, although this house will be for you, if the project succeeds, you will build more houses in the future. It doesn't have to be true; it just has to be said. Contractors' labor charges to a general contractor should be about 50 percent less than charges to the general public for the same work. This discount is predicated on the prospect for future income from addi-

If you can't find a general contractor who can satisfy your needs, try to convince one of the contractors you wish to hire to oversee the project and advise you along the way.

tional homes to be built. Let the contractors assume you are going to build at least 5 to 10 homes per year if this first one is successful.

I have visited hundreds of construction sites, most of them my own projects. One fact remained constant across all of them: *Good work is a direct result of the hiring of good contractors.* It's common sense. If you want an inferior project, hire inferior workers; do just the opposite if you want a well-built project.

It's common sense. If you want an inferior project, hire inferior workers.

There are thousands of skilled workers out there, but there are few conscientious skilled workers. You want to hire contractors who not only produce quality results but genuinely care about the jobs they perform.

Most professional contractors have their names on their equipment or trucks. I stress *professional contractors* because they are the ones who are committed to their profession. They have all of the proper licenses and insurance and can provide references for their work. Their equipment will be in good condition, and they will use up-to-date methods on the job.

You will always find someone who will do the same job for less money than the other guy. Do not be fooled into accepting the lowest bid. If you hire a fly-by-night worker who works full time for someone else and independently on the side, chances are you will get exactly what you pay for: a cheap job.

The easiest way to find contractors is to visit the places where they work. Visit several small new-home construction sites. I mention small sites because you are building just one house. There is no point in contacting contractors with the equipment and labor resources to handle large projects. Their overhead is too high to let them offer competitive prices to a small builder.

Locate the projects that have from 1 to 30 homes under construction. If you are building a large custom home, go to other custom-home sites. If you are building a mid-range home, find comparable projects. And if you are just starting out with a modest home, locate similar developments.

Contractors will qualify in their own areas of expertise. If you require custom detailed work, do not hire a starter or mid-range contractor. That person will probably not have the experience to qualify for the work you need. On the other hand, don't hire a custom contractor and pay him or her custom prices to do a standard job.

If you visit a job site and the workers are busy, not on a break or lunch hour, don't enter the project and disturb them. They are there to make a living; they are being paid for their time, and time is money in the contracting business. You may see contractors' signs scattered about, and you will see their trucks showing their logos and phone numbers. If you can, leave business cards with the job superintendent. Ask the superintendent's permission to contact the contractors; you may be allowed onto the site to speak with the workers. If not, write down as many phone numbers as you can find. The best time to call a contractor is in the early evening after dinner or in the early morning after 6 A.M.

If you visit a site where only a few homes are being built, you should be able to speak with the contractors without a superintendent on the job. Locate the contractor's job boss or the owner of the company. Leave your business card with the workers. If no one is on the site, leave several business cards in places where the contractors must see them. Write on the back of each card that you are building a house and would appreciate a return call.

You can also find contractor names in the Yellow Pages, but I always prefer to visit the construction sites. I can see that the contractors are working, and I have a chance to check out their work.

If you have the opportunity to meet with the developer or the owner of a new house, ask him or her to step out of listening range of the workers and ask which contractors have done satisfactory work. The person may prefer not to say, and that is okay, but if you can elicit recommendations from the general contractor, developer, or home owner, you will save valuable time in your search.

If several homes in the development are completed and the owners have moved in, knock on a few doors and ask whether the owners are satisfied with their homes. Have there been problems, and have the contractors returned to make repairs within a reasonable time? If there have been problems, what were they? Who was responsible? Try to obtain as much information as possible without being too forceful. Explain that you don't

They are there to make a living; they are being paid for their time, and time is money in the contracting business.

If no one is on the site, leave several business cards in places where the contractors must see them.

want to intrude but are building your own home and would appreciate any help you can get.

Interview the Contractors

When you meet with contractors, whether on the job or at their homes or offices, be truthful. Let them know that you are building your own home to try to save money and get the home of your dreams. They will know that you are not a professional general contractor. It is better to be honest from the beginning than to try to bluff your way through.

Most contractors are just working people trying to make a living. They don't appreciate someone who attempts to fool them. Most of them will try to help you achieve your goal if you work with them on their own level. If they like you, they will recommend other contractors who they know will do good work. They may also recommend certain suppliers who provide good materials at reasonable prices.

The Excavator

Provide each contractor with a check print or a plot plan and a materials list. The excavation contractor *(excavator)* will need a copy of the plot plan showing the location of the house and the locations of the well or water line and the septic or sewer line. This contractor will need a check print of the foundation size and depth to determine the amount of excavating to be done for the house. The excavator will also want to walk the site to determine what other site work, such as tree or brush removal, may be necessary. If you will install a septic system, you will need to supply a detailed plan of the system from your engineer.

The Mason

The foundation contractor *(mason)* will need a copy of the foundation check print showing the length, width, and depth. The print should also show the points where the water and sewer lines will enter the house and the

It is better to be honest from the beginning than to try to bluff your way through.

locations of any interior floor drains. The mason will have to know the size of the house and the number of kitchens and bathrooms to determine the amount of plumbing required. He or she will need to know whether your foundation will be a partial or full-in-ground basement and what type of material you want to use. There are concrete block and poured concrete foundations, and in some areas, wooden foundations are used. I prefer poured concrete or concrete block walls. Poured concrete is much stronger and can be poured in one day, but it is difficult to cut through if you need to. Concrete block is easier to work with, but the foundation may take several days to complete. Poured concrete may cost a little more.

I prefer poured concrete or concrete block walls.

The Plumber

You need to inform the *plumber* about the kind of heating and air-conditioning system you will install; the number and types of toilets, sinks, tabs, and showers in the bathrooms; the number and types of sinks in the kitchen; the number and locations of exterior water spigots; and any other plumbing features such as floor drains, wet bars, or water lines to refrigerator ice makers.

The Electrician

The *electrician* needs to know what level of power you want installed. A minimum of 200 amps is recommended. If you install less capacity, you may find that you lack power as you add equipment to the house or use power tools. To upgrade later is expensive.

Go over the check print with the electrician to indicate where you would like the wall switches located and what type you would prefer. Most local codes require a wall outlet every 8 linear feet in a room. If you want more outlets, now is the time to say so. Electricians love to combine several rooms on the same circuit to save money. Because you are ordering 200-amp service, you should have sufficient room in the electrical-panel box for additional circuits and circuit breakers.

Make sure that each bathroom and the garage is serviced by its own circuit. The kitchen, baths, and garage should also have several circuits with GFI

Electricians love to combine several rooms on the same circuit to save money.

109

(ground-fault interrupter) circuit breakers installed. A GFI circuit breaker has a sensor built in to detect when the circuit is overloaded, such as with a hair dryer or frypan that draws a lot of power. If the circuit becomes overloaded, the GFI breaker will trip and open the circuit, turning off the outlet before it overheats. Be sure to plan ample outlets in the kitchen for your coffee maker, toaster oven, answering machine, television, frypans, and any other appliances you will use there.

The electrician will need to know the size and type of heating and air-conditioning systems you will install, as well as the number and types of ceiling fans or ceiling light fixtures, bath vanity lights, and kitchen counter lights. What type of range, refrigerator, range vent fan, and microwave oven have you chosen? How many and what kind of exterior door lights or spotlights do you want? Will you install a garage door opener? Will the washer and dryer be gas or electric? How about driveway exterior or lawn lights? Heated-vent fans in the bathrooms are nice, and how about those new pressure-sensitive wall switches that glow in the dark? How about dedicated circuits for home computers?

Be careful! Contractors can be very helpful when you are planning a home, but they are also in business to make money and will not hesitate to sell you upgrade items. You may find that you can purchase all of your light fixtures at a local building materials outlet for much less than the electrician would charge you for the identical items. The same holds true for all of your appliances and even your plumbing fixtures. I will cover materials purchasing later in this chapter.

The Framer

The framing contractor (*framer*) will need a detailed print of the house. Ask the framer to work up a *framing-materials list* for you. This contractor will know how many two-by-fours and two-by-tens you will need, how many sheets of plywood for the flooring, and how many sheets for the exterior sheathing. The sheathing (see Figure 6.1 in Chapter 6) is used to wrap the exterior of the house; the siding will be installed over the sheathing. You may find

Be careful! Contractors can be very helpful when you are planning a home, but they are also in business to make money and will not hesitate to sell you upgrade items.

110

that your climate requires heavy insulation and that you will want to use insulated sheathing.

The framer will also tell you how many pounds of nails will be required and the number and type of joist hangers you will need. You will take this list to the materials suppliers to obtain your estimates.

When construction begins, you will need to specify what size windows, doors, and garage doors you want. In order to install the subfloor, the framer will need to know where the carpet and tile floors will be and what type of subfloor you require. I recommend at least a 3/4-inch tongue-and-groove plywood subfloor. The tongue-and-groove feature allows one piece to slip into the groove of the next, marrying them together to prevent slipping and squeaking. Tell the framer that you want the subfloors glued and screwed into place to prevent loosening, warping, and squeaking as the house ages. Also, you need to make sure the house is well vented.

If you will use a wooden siding such as cedar, the framer will need to know the type and size of the material. The same holds true for the roof: If it is wood, the framer must know the size and type.

The Sider

If you are installing masonry, vinyl, or aluminum siding, you will hire a separate siding contractor (*sider*) for that part of the project. The sider will need a copy of the check print to determine the exterior square footage of the house. Many siding contractors also install roofing. It is better to hire one contractor who does as many jobs as possible than to hire a separate contractor for each job. The contractor will have more work, you should be able to save money because the contractor will be paid for more work, and the job will be completed faster because the contractor will be on the job for each phase.

The Roofer

If the sider does not also install roofing, you will hire a *roofer*. The roofer needs a check print to measure the square footage of the roof area. Roofing and siding are

Ask the framer to work up a framing-materials list for you.

It is better to hire one contractor who does as many jobs as possible than to hire a separate contractor for each job.

111

usually installed by the *square*—each 100 square feet. A square of roofing equals 100 square feet of surface area, including all overhangs. You will buy the roofing by the square, and the roofer will charge by the square for installation. To determine the cost of labor, the roofer also needs to know the type of roofing materials you will use. Make sure the roofer also installs any soffit (overhang) material, if required, and also *flashing* between the various roof levels where the sections of roof meet. Flashing material is used to fill the gaps between roof levels or walls and is usually nailed down and sealed with asphalt. You will also install flashing where a roof meets a wall. Flashing will probably be aluminum, but you can also use copper or other upgrade materials for a custom appearance.

The price the roofer charges will depend on the material used and the pitch of the roof. If the roof has a steep pitch, extra labor will be required, and the job will cost more.

The Insulation Contractor

The *insulation contractor* will charge by the square-foot measurements of the interior of the house, including all exterior walls. The calculation will include all ceilings and floors that are exposed to unheated areas.

Dead air is a great insulator. Almost all forms of insulation are premised on this fact. The most popular form of wall and ceiling insulation used today is the *fiberglass batt*. The fiberglass is formed into extremely fine fibers, almost like human hair, and cut into sections to form *batts* of various sizes.

When I was building new homes in the late 1970s in southern New York State, the federal insulation requirements were as follows: walls—R-11, equivalent to $3^1/2$ inches of fiberglass; ceilings—R-19, equivalent to $6^1/4$ inches of fiberglass; and floors (basement ceilings)—R-11. (*R* designates ability to resist heat or cold infiltration.) The most common material used for wall construction at that time was the two-by-four stud.

When the new energy codes were enacted early in 1976, partly because of the rise in oil prices and the nation's burgeoning environmental awareness, the re-

Make sure the roofer also installs any soffit (overhang) material, if required, and also flashing between the various roof levels where the sections of roof meet.

Dead air is a great insulator. Almost all forms of insulation are premised on this fact.

112

quirements changed. The minimum wall requirement increased to R-19, the floor stayed at R-11, and the ceiling increased to R-30, which is equivalent to 9 inches of fiberglass. To achieve the increase in (R) factors without increasing the dimensions of the lumber itself and thereby substantially boosting the cost of the house, several manufacturers introduced *insulated sheathing*. (Sheathing (see Figure 6.1 in Chapter 6) is the material used to wrap the exterior walls of the house to cut down on air infiltration and moisture.) Until then the most common sheathing was plywood, which was itself wrapped in tar paper.

Insulated sheathing consisted of two layers of aluminized foil with a polyfoam insulation product sandwiched between them. The insulated sheathing had an average (R) factor of 5 and, when added to the R-11 wall insulation, brought the overall wall (R) factor to R-16. To achieve the balance of insulation needed, builders' engineers calculated the (R) factors of the siding, the foil backing, the paper vapor barriers on the fiberglass, and the Sheetrock on the interior walls of the house to reach a total of R-19. This formula was debatable, but it was accepted by building inspectors.

Many builders, preferring to keep it simple and to make their products more appealing, started advertising houses constructed with two-by-six exterior walls with full-batt 6¼ inch (R-19) fiberglass insulation. This form of building became very popular with buyers because the two-by-six wall sounded much more substantial than a two-by-four wall. It remains a popular form of construction today.

The exterior walls do not hold up much more than the siding because the actual structural lumber used in building the frame takes almost all the stress. The two-by-ten floor joist with R-11 has remained, and ceiling joists have increased to two-by-eight to accommodate the 9½ inches needed to achieve the required R-30. Structural lumber, used to create the frame of a house where the most stress is exerted, has also changed in recent years because of the *forced growth* of lumber. In this process, trees are chemically treated to grow faster; this makes them less dense, hence—weaker. It is common now to see the dimensions of lumber increase to take added stress–

The exterior walls do not hold up much more than the siding because the actual structural lumber used in building the frame takes almost all the stress.

for example, floor joists increasing from two-by-eight to two-by-ten or even larger.

In older homes, built in the late 1800s to the early 1900s, it is not uncommon to see nothing but a space between the walls to create dead air. Sometimes that space was filled with hay or even horsehair. To compensate for the lack of insulation, a variety of cellulose insulation products can be blown in from outside to fill the space. The overall key to a well-insulated home is to stop the heat or cold from coming in while you stop the cold or heat from going out.

Don't Seal It Completely

To seal the house completely against any air infiltration whatsoever is dangerous.

To seal the house completely against any air infiltration whatsoever is dangerous. A house must breathe just like you and I. I have seen new homes whose owners wanted the inside of the exterior walls entirely lined with plastic to seal out the cold. However, the plastic not only sealed out the cold; it sealed in all the moisture generated in washing, cooking, showering, and so on. The interior walls of the house remained damp and mold began to grow because they never dried out.

You also must breathe while inside your house, especially during the heating season in colder climates. The interior of a house produces all kinds of pollutants such as carpet fibers, Sheetrock particles, carbon dioxide from human breathing and from the heating system, chemicals from cleaning fluids, and more. Everything breaks down over time, and we need a certain amount of fresh air inside a structure to replace the stale air we create. Insulate all you want, but do not seal up the house completely.

Ventilation

If this hot, moist air cannot escape, condensation can build up and rot the roof rafters and ceiling joists.

In homes constructed since the 1970s, a common practice has been to install a *continuous-ridge vent*. This type of vent, made of metal or plastic, runs continuously along the very top or ridge of the roof to allow hot, moist air accumulated in the attic to escape. If this hot, moist air cannot escape, condensation can build up and rot the roof rafters and ceiling joists.

MATCHING CONTRACTORS WITH PRICES

In areas of the Southeast, where it is hot during the day and the temperature drops dramatically overnight, condensation can build up quickly in the warm attic space if the air is not allowed to vent. I have seen homes in which moisture stains were visible on the ceiling and inspection of the attic revealed condensation forming on the tips of the roofing nails that protruded through the roof sheathing and dripped down like rain onto the insulation. This phenomenon was due to a lack of proper ventilation.

If a home does not have a continuous vent, it may have vents installed just under the peak of the roof on each end of the house. This type of vent is called a *gable-end vent* or *end vent*. In contemporary-style homes with many peaks and valleys in the rooflines, you may find a variety of venting systems. If your home has a cathedral or tray-type ceiling, make sure the insulation in that high ceiling is not installed tight against the underside of the roof sheathing. If the area is not vented or air is not allowed to pass between the roof and the insulation, condensation will form where most of the heat accumulates, and the wood will rot. In newer homes, a Styrofoam tray known as an *eave baffle* is installed between the roof and the insulation to allow hot, moist air to flow to the roof vents.

You will achieve enough air flow around the doors, windows, and exterior electrical outlets simply by opening and closing the doors on a regular basis. Fiberglass insulation comes in batts of various sizes with (R) factors from R-11 to R-38. I believe in at least an R-19 exterior wall and R-38 in the ceiling in any area of the country. The insulation not only keeps out the cold but retains the air-conditioned cool in areas of extreme summer heat. Fiberglass insulation combined with thermopane windows and insulated exterior doors should keep your home comfortable and energy efficient, with a payback over time.

Windows and Doors

You should consider using *double-glazed* windows, in which two panes of glass are evident. A double-glazed (often called *thermopane*) window is often a full glass window with the window grills built on the inside of the two panes, or

The insulation not only keeps out the cold but retains the air-conditioned cool in areas of extreme summer heat.

115

the grills may be attached separately to the inside of the window. One of the most efficient insulators is *dead-air space*. Almost all types of insulators use this principle. In thermopane windows, the manufacturer creates a dead-air space between the two panes of glass by installing a rubber gasket around the panes and marrying them together, thereby sealing the windows from air infiltration around the panes.

The two worst areas for air infiltration and heat loss are windows and doors. Most air leakage problems can be solved or reduced by use of a silicone sealant or weather stripping.

The Sheetrocker

The Sheetrock installer (known as the "rocker" in the trades), like the insulation installer, will measure the interior square footage of the entire house, including all closets and storage areas and the garage. The garage will need a fire-code (fire-retarding) Sheetrock that meets local and federal code requirements for garage spaces where oil, paint, and gasoline are stored. The bathrooms and kitchen should have water-resistant Sheetrock to handle areas where excess moisture is generated. If you plan to install an oil or gas-fired heating system, you should frame in the furnace area and seal it with fire-code Sheetrock. Install ductwork to ensure that the area is well vented, with sufficient fresh air provided to the heating system.

The balance of the house will use standard Sheetrock. I recommend Sheetrock at least $1/2$ inch to $5/8$ inch thick to prevent sagging. The contractor should apply at least two coats of spackle (*mud*) with metal corner beads to complete the project. The mud should be sanded and ready for painting.

You may want to finish the walls in the garage. This is not common in the eastern states, but it is standard practice in the West. Finished walls look nicer than bare Sheetrock with strips of wall tape showing.

Again, try to find a contractor who will provide more than one service. Many Sheetrock installers also install insulation. You should save money, and the job will progress at a faster pace.

The two worst areas for air infiltration and heat loss are windows and doors.

Again, try to find a contractor who will provide more than one service.

The Painter

The *painter* will also measure the interior and exterior of the house and charge either by the square foot or by the room. Talk with the painter about the quality of the paint. You will want a washable latex in the kitchen, baths, and laundry rooms. You may want a flat latex for the balance of the house. Flat white latex is common in the eastern states.

The painter may charge extra for colors. Remember, time is money: If the job will take more time, expect to pay for it. The painter will also apply stain for any woodwork, either interior or exterior. Obtain a separate price for each phase. How much for interior painting? How much for exterior? How much for staining? You may decide to do some of the painting yourself to save money.

The painter may charge extra for colors.

The Trimmer

The trim installer (*trimmer*) will install the kitchen cabinets, all floor and door trim, and all of the doors. Treat this contractor with kindness. One of the *finish contractors* (no, that doesn't mean they are from Scandinavia) who will make your home look its best, the trimmer can perform miracles when patching other contractors' mistakes. The trimmer will measure all areas for floor or ceiling trim and will charge by the *linear foot*. He or she will calculate the number of doors (interior and exterior) and cabinets and offer a price.

The trimmer can perform miracles when patching other contractors' mistakes.

The Tile Installer

The *tile installer* will measure the areas for tile and charge by the square foot. This person is also a finish contractor, and you want a good job.

The Carpet Installer

The *carpet installer* will measure areas to be carpeted and charge by the *square yard*. This is another finish contractor, so be nice.

When you locate a carpet supplier, ask about the cost of installing an upgrade (thicker) carpet pad. Upgrade pads usually do not cost much more than standard ones, and the thicker pad makes the floor feel luxurious, even if you use an inexpensive carpet. If you plan to use an upgrade pad, make sure you let the trimmer know. He or she might have to cut the interior doors a little shorter to prevent them from rubbing on the carpet when opened.

The only contractor remaining is probably you.

The only contractor remaining is probably you. You will probably be on the job during each phase of construction, making a pest of yourself by asking hundreds of questions and taking up valuable work time. If you do, expect to pay for the privilege. You can be nice to the contractors, but don't waste their time. If you have hired a general contractor or another contractor to oversee the project, most of your contact should be with that person. Let the people working on site do their jobs.

Accepting Bids from Contractors

You have provided all the contractors with check prints to enable them to estimate their costs and profit margins. They should have access to your engineer to resolve any questions they may have regarding the design and the needed materials. They should have visited the site to establish the time required for their crews to move to and from the job site, and they should be ready to offer you bids for their work.

It is not uncommon for a contractor to underbid competitors just to win the contract.

Be cautious! It is not uncommon for a contractor to underbid competitors just to win the contract. The contractor builds language into the bid or contract that allows him or her to charge more for ambiguous areas of the job.

One favorite of the excavation contractor is to quote you a price for the job and charge by the hour. Let's say the bid for all of the excavation work is $15,000, calculated at $65 per hour for the backhoe, $60 per hour for the D4 bulldozer, and $85 per hour for the trackhoe. How many hours of machine time equal $15,000? If the contractor does not break the total charges down, you have no way of controlling the amount of time charged.

MATCHING CONTRACTORS WITH PRICES

If you are charged by the hour and the job takes longer than the contractor calculated, you will be charged for the additional time and could run up thousands of dollars in extra costs. This approach is known as a *cost-plus contract*. The contractor offers a bid at an estimated cost plus additional charges for any work that exceeds the estimate. Subcontractor contracts and agreements are covered in Chapter 8.

The only situation in which you may have to allow for additional charges is if the excavation contractor requires a *rock clause* in the agreement. As I explained in Chapter 4, hidden, subsurface rock may be present, and the excavator will want to be protected in the event rock removal is necessary. The rock clause allows the contractor to charge extra for rock removal. You have the right to place a dollar limit on the amount charged. If rock is encountered and appears to be expensive to remove, you may have to relocate your foundation away from the rock or lose part of the foundation by building a concrete slab over the rock area.

The framer can come up with daily problems that require changes in material and added labor costs if you let this happen. The roofer and the sider should have stable costs and expense estimates. The insulator and Sheetrocker might add 20 percent to their bills for waste. The painter should know the costs well enough not to overcharge.

Basically, with the exception of a few contractors who leave gray areas open in their agreements, most contractors will stick to their original bids. If you don't allow yourself to be talked into too many changes as the job progresses, you should complete the project within your budget.

Bids may be presented on formal letterhead, on hand-written invoices, or even on plain paper. As long as the contractor signs his or her name at the bottom, it is okay to accept the bid. Meet with the contractors in your office, in your home, or at the job site. Let them come to you. Establish from the beginning who is in charge and who pays the bills, but *accomplish this gently.* There is nothing so easily offended as a contractor's ego. You must be firm yet friendly at the same time.

Establish from the beginning who is in charge and who pays the bills, but accomplish this gently.

Review each bid thoroughly with the contractor to avoid misunderstandings. Explain that if any portion of the bid is not agreed to in writing, it will not be binding. Try to obtain at least three bids for each phase of the project. Compare these bids against your budget and the cost estimates you received from your engineer. On the basis of your own assessment of each contractor and the strength of each bid, make your choices to hire.

When negotiating with each contractor, try to obtain his or her best price for the job. There is usually some negotiating room in each bid. If you can reach the negotiated price, ask the contractor if he or she would allow additional discounts for green cash. One fellow said to me many years ago, "Credit is great and checks are good, but cash is king." You should be able to negotiate prices at least 10 percent lower for cash payments. When the contractor has reached the bottom price, ask if he or she would perform a few more jobs on site, such as cleaning up after each phase or overseeing a certain phase for you, in compensation for the cash payments.

There is usually some negotiating room in each bid.

Once you have selected your contractors, let them know that you will be happy to pay them on time as long as they continue to perform the work in a timely and professional manner and according to the terms of their contracts. Review your timetable with the contractors to schedule the work. Tell them that you will be in contact with them weekly to firm up the construction schedule, and allow them sufficient time to schedule their crews for your project.

You will have to reconfirm the timing for the availability of the construction funding (I will cover this matter in Chapter 9). Verify with your engineer that all necessary *working drawings* will be available. You will need a working set of final drawings for the house to submit to the municipality and the utility companies for all of your permits. These drawings will show all of the finished details from the foundation to the roof, including all electrical and plumbing systems. Check to see if the municipality requires separate drawings for the electrical, plumbing, heating, and air-conditioning systems. If so, you must have all of these drawings ready for submission when needed. Ask if you need to submit any additional documents, such as before-and-after topographical maps for the plot plan.

Make sure you have all required documents ready. If any are missing, your project will be delayed until you can supply them. The landowner (assuming you haven't paid cash in full for the lot) will be waiting. The bank will be waiting to fund the loan at the agreed-upon interest rate. The contractors will be ready to start work according to the schedule you demanded. If you cannot start on time, you may lose certain contractors to other projects, and you will have to begin your search again.

Construction Costs

There are two categories of costs in construction: *hard costs,* for material and labor, and *soft costs,* for everything that is not material and labor.

Use a form like Table 7.1 to keep track of the bids for hard costs that are submitted to you.

The next round of bids will come from the material suppliers. Conduct the same search for material suppliers as you did for contractors. Check other projects, and locate the suppliers' trucks and drivers. Write down the names of the suppliers, and ask the drivers whom you should contact in their companies.

Visit several lumber yards, carrying along several copies of your check prints. At each one, ask to speak with the person in charge of builder contracts. Tell that person what your goal is, and give him or her your business card. Explain that you want to sign up as a general contractor customer, that your financing has been approved, and that this will be your first house. Say that if you are successful, you hope to build many more. This statement may or may not be true, but if the supplier feels that you will bring repeat business, you will probably be offered better prices than someone who is only going to build one house. Experience has taught me that a general contractor should receive a discount of at least 30 percent off the retail price for all lumber materials. The prices of windows, exterior doors, and interior trim (including that for the kitchen) should be discounted 20 percent or more. When you estimate that these materials

Make sure you have all required documents ready.

Write down the names of the suppliers, and ask the drivers whom you should contact in their companies.

121

TABLE 7.1 Hard Costs for Labor

Labor bids	Amount of bid	Negotiated bid
Excavator:		
Bid no. 1 (name of company)	$	$
Bid no. 2 (name of company)		
Bid no. 3 (name of company)		
Mason:		
Bid no. 1 (name of company)	$	$
Bid no. 2 (name of company)		
Bid no. 3 (name of company)		
Plumber:		
Bid no. 1 (name of company)	$	$
Bid no. 2 (name of company)		
Bid no. 3 (name of company)		
Electrician:		
Bid no. 1 (name of company)	$	$
Bid no. 2 (name of company)		
Bid no. 3 (name of company)		
Framer:		
Bid no. 1 (name of company)	$	$
Bid no. 2 (name of company)		
Bid no. 3 (name of company)		
Sider:		
Bid no. 1 (name of company)	$	$
Bid no. 2 (name of company)		
Bid no. 3 (name of company)		
Roofer:		
Bid no. 1 (name of company)	$	$
Bid no. 2 (name of company)		
Bid no. 3 (name of company)		
Insulator:		
Bid no. 1 (name of company)	$	$
Bid no. 2 (name of company)		
Bid no. 3 (name of company)		

TABLE 7.1 *continued*

Sheetrocker:

Bid no. 1 (name of company)	$	$
Bid no. 2 (name of company)		
Bid no. 3 (name of company)		

Painter:

Bid no. 1 (name of company)	$	$
Bid no. 2 (name of company)		
Bid no. 3 (name of company)		

Trimmer:

Bid no. 1 (name of company)	$	$
Bid no. 2 (name of company)		
Bid no. 3 (name of company)		

Tile installer: (ceramic/vinyl)

Bid no. 1 (name of company)	$	$
Bid no. 2 (name of company)		
Bid no. 3 (name of company)		

Carpet installer:

Bid no. 1 (name of company)	$	$
Bid no. 2 (name of company)		
Bid no. 3 (name of company)		

Total labor costs:	$	$

will account for about 50 percent of the materials cost of your project, you can see the savings.

Table 7.2 is a sample checklist for the materials hard costs.

Review the completed list of materials costs with your suppliers. Try to find a supplier who will furnish more than one product; preferably, he or she can supply materials for most of the job. You will receive better prices and service when most of the project can be coordinated through one supplier. Also, it is easier to track down and correct mistakes when you have a limited number of people to deal with.

Review the completed list of materials costs with your suppliers. Try to find a supplier who will furnish more than one product.

TABLE 7.2 Hard Costs for Materials

	Materials	Sales tax	Delivery	Total
Concrete/footings	$	$	$	$
Concrete/walls				
Concrete/slab				
Lumber/deck, floor				
Lumber/walls				
Windows				
Exterior doors				
Garage doors				
Lumber/roof				
Siding				
Tubs/showers				
Roofing				
Insulation				
Sheetrock				
Paint				
Tile				
Trim				
Bath fixtures				
Kitchen cabinets				
Interior doors				
Hardware				
Appliances				
Total hard costs				$

If a supplier's prices are in line, ask to sign an agreement that these prices will not rise during the course of your project. The suppliers will probably ask that you sign personally for your purchases. Because personal signatures carry certain risks if the job cannot be completed for any reason, such as illness or accident, you should try to avoid personal signatures if you can. The agreement should also state that the supplier agrees to have your material in the warehouse according to your construction schedule and to deliver the material according to your needs, given proper advance notice. Many a job is held up when the builder calls for certain materials and the supplier is out of stock and the delivery truck is late. Make sure the suppliers agree to stock all of your needed materials in advance.

TABLE 7.3 Total Soft Costs

Attorney's fee	$
Engineer's fee	$
Surveyor's fee	$
Permit/fees	$
Bank application fees	$
Bank commitment fees	$
Estimated closing costs	$
Deposits	$
Estimated interest on construction loan	$
Total soft costs	$

Table 7.3 lists the *soft costs*—professional fees, bank charges, and permit fees. Review these costs, and match the total to your initial budget to see if your numbers will work.

Add your total soft costs and hard costs to arrive at the total estimate. Your engineer can verify the range of hard costs, and your attorney and banker can verify the estimated soft costs. If all of these numbers are in line with your financial capabilities and you still want to proceed, Chapter 9 will help you structure the financing.

Add your total soft costs and hard costs to arrive at the total estimate.

CHAPTER
8

Preparing
Contractor
Agreements

A Word of Warning

Make sure that any agreement with any contractor that you sign and approve is subject to your obtaining the financing to purchase the building lot and the issuance of all permits required to complete the project within your budget. Also, make sure that all contractor agreements specify completion times for the work and that the contractors acknowledge in writing that they will be held responsible for any delays caused by their failure to complete their respective jobs on time.

Bill Padding

Contractors love to find different ways to increase your costs. They will constantly approach you and mention, "You know, if we did it this way, it would make a much nicer job, and it would only cost an extra $200." I mentioned in Chapter 7 that excavation contractors find ways to charge extra time onto their bills. Other contractors will also attempt to increase their income by convincing you to add extras. There is nothing wrong with this practice—I would do the same thing if I were a contractor on site—but $200 here and $200 there add up to thousands of dollars over the course of the job. If your budget doesn't allow for extra costs, just say, "Thanks for making

Make sure that any agreement with any contractor that you sign and approve is subject to your obtaining the financing to purchase the building lot and the issuance of all permits required to complete the project within your budget.

me aware of the opportunity. I wish I could, but I can't afford it."

Here's an illustration from my experience. I was involved in building a group of duplex apartment buildings in an area that had no access to a central sewer. The soil was mostly clay, and we were forced to install fill-section septic systems to service the buildings.

To make a fill-section septic system (to be discussed in Chapter 10), you create a depression in the shape of a swimming pool and fill that area with good, drainable (permeable) soil to allow the system to function. Filling this area requires a bulldozer to be on hand every day to grade out the fill as it is dumped, and as the machine moves back and forth over the loose fill, it compacts the material at the same time.

On this job, I was responsible for verifying all invoices (a partner was the on-site manager), and I wasn't shocked to see extensive charges for machine time arriving in the mail. When they continued to arrive, I wondered why. The charges seemed excessive, and I decided to visit the site. I also decided not to let anyone know that I was visiting and found an inconspicuous place to sit and watch. The trucks did in fact come and go, delivering material, and the excavator did grade out the material as agreed—except that when the trucks left the site, he turned the machine off and lit a cigarette. He was supposed to keep running the machine back and forth, compacting the fill. If the fill was not compacted mechanically, the engineer would not approve the material for installation of the system.

I decided to wait out the day just to see what the contractor would charge me for that day. Sure enough, I was charged for a full eight-hour day, when in fact the machine had actually run for about three hours. The contractor said that I was to be charged as long as the machine was on my site. I said, "If the machine was not *working* on my site, I will not pay for it." I reviewed our contract. To make a long story short, I found another, more honest contractor.

The easiest way to avoid overcharges is to *avoid the cost-plus contract*. When all bids are in and you have had the time to review them, inform the contractors that you will only sign contracts with those who agree in writing to

To make a fill-section septic system (to be discussed in Chapter 10), you create a depression in the shape of a swimming pool and fill that area with good, drainable (permeable) soil to allow the system to function.

complete their respective jobs for the prices submitted and within specific time frames. If the cost of a job increases beyond the contracted price, the contractor will have to pay the difference. This approach will weed out the contractors who intend to pick your pockets and leave you with experienced ones who know their work.

A Third, a Third, and a Third

In the eastern states, one accepted method for paying contractors has been in one-third increments as the job progressed. For example, if the contractor's bid for the job was $6,000, you would offer to pay $2,000 when the rough-in work was completed, another $2,000 when the equipment was installed, and the $2,000 balance when the job was totally finished.

This method of payment allows the contractor to pay for labor and materials as the job progresses, and it can give you control over the quality of the job. If you find a problem with a contractor's work, you can withhold all or a portion of the payment until the problem is corrected.

Contractors make their money with time on the job. Most contractors, with the exception of plumbers or electricians, who can provide materials, have invested only in their trucks and tools. They offer their skills and their time, with someone else providing the materials. By accepting as many jobs as they can get, they generate a constant level of work and income. Understandably, if one project is held up by bad weather or lack of material, the contractor wants to be able to move to another job and still make an income. The problem is that contractors habitually accept more work than they can physically accommodate to keep that money flowing in.

One can't serve two masters at the same time. If a contractor moves to another job, your project may be delayed until he or she returns. If you continually pay in full for each phase of the job, you are providing no incentive to return and complete the job on time because the contractor is making more money elsewhere.

In the eastern states, one accepted method for paying contractors has been in one-third increments as the job progressed.

131

A good tactic is to hold back at least 10 percent from each payment. Find some problem that you would like corrected. Blame the bank for shortchanging you on your construction draw. Say that your engineer hasn't approved the installation yet. Say whatever you must to convince the contractor that you cannot pay in full. If the contractor fears losing money—even by moving to another job—he or she will return in a reasonable time to complete your job. If the contractor doesn't return, hire someone else and keep the 10 percent holdback.

Another incremental payment formula is 45–45–10. This formula is more generous but allows you to hold 10 percent for at least two weeks at the end of the job to ensure that all problems are corrected. You might build this 10-percent feature into the one-third-increment formula for a 30–30–30–10 payment schedule.

If you expect contractors to do good work and be conscientious, they must be paid on time.

If you expect contractors to do good work and be conscientious, they must be paid on time. If you do not pay your workers on time, they simply won't show up on time, if they show up at all. However, experience has taught me that once contractors have been paid in full, they disappear quickly to some unknown secret contractor place and spend their money on stuff.

One considerable problem in the industry is getting a contractor to return to correct a defect. Nothing is perfect in construction. More than 40,000 components are installed into each house, and every house will have some problems. Each problem must be dealt with quickly before it balloons into a bigger one. Let's say that you find a slow leak in the cold-water intake line under the kitchen sink—a small drip that shouldn't take long to repair. You paid the plumber to install the water line correctly. You call, and you are assured that someone will come by the next day to fix the leak. No one shows up. Meanwhile, that small drip is filling the bucket you placed under it and is growing into a bigger drip. If the problem is not repaired soon, there may be damage to the base cabinet. Who will pay to replace the cabinet? If you can do the repair, do it and admonish the contractor. If you paid the contractor in full, good luck. If you held back at least 10 percent, I'm sure someone will show up to repair the leak. See how it works?

Protect Yourself

In the western states, it is more difficult to hold back payments. Contractors have more power there than in the East. If a contractor is not paid for work done, *even if the work is faulty,* he or she has the right immediately to file a mechanic's lien against the project. A *mechanic's lien* is a legal paper filed with the county clerk documenting an unpaid debt.

The filing of a lien creates a *cloud on the title* for the property. You purchased the property with a *free and marketable title, clear of all encumbrances* (see Chapter 5). The lender will require that the title be clear before advancing further funds or closing the permanent mortgage. The best advise is to photograph the disputed job. Try to obtain an affidavit from another contractor or your project manager that the contractor did not fulfill the contract. *Pay the contractor to clear the title;* you can sue the contractor in civil court to recover your money. Get your attorney's advise on any such dispute.

In the eastern states, you can *bond* the lien, allowing the project to continue, and fight it out with the contractor in court later. You may obtain a bond from your insurance company.

To avoid these conflicts, many states require that contractors and material suppliers sign an affidavit or release after each payment that provides proof that all invoices have been satisfied. If a contractor files a lien after signing a release, he or she can become criminally liable for damages if the lien affects the project.

Many lenders in the western states now require that a *construction management company* handle all invoices and the distribution of all monies. The management company charges from $1/2$ percent to 1 percent of each payment as a fee and acts as a third party to distribute the funds. The money will not be released to a contractor or supplier until the management company receives a release-of-lien affidavit for each invoice. Using a management company is a good way to keep control of your finances and the contractors. You will have to budget for the added expense. Meet with the management company officials and make them party to all subcontractor agree-

The lender will require that the title be clear before advancing further funds or closing the permanent mortgage.

You will have to budget for the added expense.

TABLE 8.1 Subcontractor Agreement

Owner	Contractor (company name)
	Owner's name
Address	Address
Phone	Phone
Fax	Fax
Workers' comp. insurance no.	Job address
Insurance carrier	Amount bid
	Bid good until
Payment terms	
%	Upon completion of
%	Upon completion of
%	Upon completion of
%	Upon completion of
Workers' comp. deductions	$
Amount retained upon completion	$

PROVISIONS OF AGREEMENT

All work is to be performed in a workmanlike manner according to local standards.

All materials and labor shall be warranted for a minimum of one year.

All changes requested shall be agreed to by purchase order.

Contractor agrees to maintain all required licenses and insurance, including workers' compensation and liability insurance with a minimum coverage of $500,000 per occurrence.

Any damages caused by contractor or contractor's employees is the responsibility of this contractor and shall be repaired at this contractor's expense.

Contractor is solely responsible for compensation to all employees and helpers hired by contractor.

JOB SPECIFICATIONS (describe the job)

Example:

Installation of all heating and air-conditioning equipment (brand name, model, and size of each unit), including all accessories required for the normal function of each system

Installation of all plumbing fixtures, vents, ductwork, gauges, and controls (add additional sheets such as brochures or lists of parts supplied by contractor)

This agreement is contingent upon owner's obtaining all required permits and financing to allow completion of this project as budgeted.

Work to commence on	Work to be completed on
Agreed to by	This date
Owner	Contractor

PAYMENT SCHEDULE

Date	Check no.	Amount paid	Amount due

ments. They must understand the negotiated terms of payment protect you against overpayment.

Table 8.1 illustrates a typical subcontractor agreement. A contractor agreement can be written on any form or invoice or on plain paper—anything as long as it is legible, in writing, in ink, signed, and notarized.

You need an agreement with every contractor and material supplier who is either working on the job or delivering material for the job. A typical release-of-lien form is illustrated in Figure 8.1.

While you are signing contracts, don't forget—if you are hiring a general contractor to represent you—to execute a contract with your general contractor. That

SUBCONTRACTOR RELEASE-OF-LIEN AFFIDAVIT

STATE OF:

COUNTY OF:

The undersigned personally appeared before me,

_____

Who am the duly sworn contractor working to improve the property located at

_____

Owned by: _____

Contractor certifies that all labor and materials provided by contractor are and were used in the improvement for the above property; that this contractor has been fully or partially paid the agreed contract price for said improvements; that there are no unpaid bills owing for services rendered or materials supplied; and that no person has any claim for lien for said improvements.

Seal _____ Signature _____

Sworn to and subscribed before me

this _____ day of _____ 19

_____

Notary Public

FIGURE 8.1 Subcontractor release-of-lien affidavit

TABLE 8.2   General Contractor Agreement

Owner	Contractor (company name)
	Owner's name
Address	Address
Phone	Phone
Fax	Fax
Workers' comp. insurance no.	Job address
Insurance carrier	Agreed payment
	Bid good until
PAYMENT TERMS	(payment terms may vary)
%	Upon completion of
%	Upon completion of
%	Upon completion of
%	Upon completion of
Workers' comp. deductions	$
Amount retained upon completion	$

PROVISIONS OF AGREEMENT

All work is to be performed in a workmanlike manner according to local standards.

All materials and labor shall be warranted for a minimum of one year.

All changes requested shall be agreed to by purchase order.

General contractor agrees to maintain all required licenses and insurance, including workers' compensation and liability insurance with a minimum coverage of $500,000 per occurrence. Any damage caused by contractor or contractor's employees is the responsibility of this contractor and shall be repaired at this contractor's expense.

Contractor is solely responsible for compensation to all employees and helpers hired by contractor.

Contractor agrees to provide owner with release-of-lien affidavits prior to each payment.

Contractor is responsible for obtaining all required permits and licenses.

Contractor is responsible for verifying all subcontractor permits and licenses.

Contractor will ensure the cleanliness of the project at all times.

Contractor is responsible to provide a safe working environment for all workers.

A penalty of $ _____ per day shall be charged to contractor if contractor defaults on this agreement or stops work before the project is completed.

Owner reserves the right to hire a replacement general contractor to complete contractor's contract in the event contractor defaults.

Additional work for rock removal or poor soil conditions shall be negotiated separately.

This agreement is contingent upon owner's obtaining required permits and financing to allow completion of the project as budgeted.

JOB SPECIFICATIONS   (describe the job)

TABLE 8.2 *continued*

Example:

Contractor shall be responsible for the completion of the entire project according to the agreed-on time schedule.

Contractor shall act as overall manager, scheduling all labor and material deliveries.

Contractor is responsible to complete the project within the financial budget set forth by the owner.

Work to commence on or about	Work to be completed on or about	
Agreed by	This date	
Owner	Contractor	
PAYMENT SCHEDULE	This date	
Date Check no.	Amount paid	Amount due

agreement is similar to the subcontractor's agreement but the content of the agreed-upon terms will differ.

Table 8.2 is an example of a general contractor's (GC) agreement.

If, instead of engaging a general contractor, you have simply persuaded one of the subcontractors to help oversee the project, it will probably be difficult to lock that person into a binding contract. Try to have him or her sign a simple agreement that spells out responsibilities and payment requirements. At least you will have something in writing if problems develop.

The agreement could be as simple as the following illustration.

At least you will have something in writing if problems develop.

Construction Agreement

By and between John Jones as owner
   and
Paul Smith as manager.

Paul Smith agrees to help John Jones complete the new house to be built at (000 street, city, state).

Paul Smith agrees to use his experience in the construction business to act as project manager and oversee all phases of construction, advise John Jones on the hiring of subcontractors, and advise on the purchasing of materials.

Paul Smith agrees that he shall accept a 5-percent override of total costs as compensation for this additional service.

This simple agreement offers you some protection in the event of a problem. Paul Smith acknowledges that he has appropriate experience and agrees to manage the project for compensation. Check with your attorney for clarification. In my eyes, Paul has just become the general contractor.

What about Insurance?

Meet with an insurance agent, preferably a commercial agent who works in the new-construction field. You will need *builder's risk insurance*. Builder's risk protects you in the event of an accident on the job. Construction is a dangerous business. People are scrambling over the job site shooting nails, digging holes, and walking through the skeleton on the roof rafters with nothing between them and the basement floor. It is not uncommon for someone to fall or have a nail shot through the hand by a nail gun. You may have done nothing to cause this accident, but if the injured worker will be out of work for a long time, you may be sued.

I heard of one instance many years ago where a painter was working on the roof of a new apartment building. He stepped back to admire his work and accidentally stepped off the roof. He fell two stories and broke his back. This was clearly not the developer's or the general contractor's fault—the man stepped off the roof—but the owners were sued anyway and lost to the contractor. The contractor based his suit on unsafe ground conditions, which were the responsibility of the developer. The painter hobbled into court with his three kids and won $2,000,000, $500,000 more than the developer's insurance coverage. I feel sorry for the contractor, but it was clearly his mistake. There is no such thing as safe ground conditions on a construction site.

Take your insurance agent's advice, and buy the maximum coverage. The cost is a tiny fraction of what a lawsuit could cost. Your agent will also recommend that each contractor and material supplier provide you with proof of coverage for workers' compensation and liability. *Make sure to obtain all insurance binders before anyone begins work.*

PREPARING CONTRACTOR AGREEMENTS

Another trick of subcontractors is to agree to provide proof of insurance and then begin to work on the site. You continue to ask, they continue to agree, and you never see the proof because they never purchased the insurance. A good way to break them of this habit is to hold back enough money from their initial payments to purchase the insurance for them. Your contracts with them require them to provide the insurance, and there should be no arguments. If a subcontractor argues about this, consider hiring another one. If you have a manager or general contractor representing you, let that individual explain the situation to the subs.

CHAPTER
9

Structuring the Financing

Understand Loan Ratios

By now, you should have in hand a good estimate of your total costs. You have been prequalified by the lender. You have located the building lot and signed a contract subject to your finalizing the numbers, receiving your engineer's approval, having soil tests done if required, securing all required permits, and obtaining the necessary financing to buy the lot and complete the project as budgeted. It is time to structure the financing.

You are ready to approach your lender. Remember what you learned in Chapter 1 regarding approval ratios and various interest rates. You can save valuable time if you have decided on a lender and the lender already has copies of your check print and plot plan. If that is not the case, give the lender a copy of the working drawings (they should be completed by now) and a copy of the plot plan. The lender's *appraiser* will have to review these items to give the lender a *market value* of the completed project. An *appraisal* is a means to arrive at an *estimate* of fair market value for a property, as defined by an appraiser, as of a specific time and for a specific purpose. An appraiser is a professional trained to verify the value of a property using several different formulas to arrive at the fair market value. In your case the appraiser must estimate the fair market value as if the project were already com-

You are ready to approach your lender.

143

Although you are charged for the appraisal, the appraiser works for the lender, who is a repeat customer.

pleted. *Although you are charged for the appraisal, the appraiser works for the lender, who is a repeat customer.*

When money is plentiful, lenders need to get their money on the street quickly to begin earning profits. Under those conditions, you will find it a little easier to qualify for financing, and the appraiser will be a little more lenient with the appraised value of property. However, when money is tight or the local market is in decline, lenders become more conservative with customers' qualifications, and the appraiser, hired by the lender (and paid by you), will tend to be more conservative with the appraised value.

Depending on the local market, if the appraisal for the home you plan comes in substantially less than the values for comparable properties, feel free to question that appraisal and possibly demand that a second one be performed by another appraiser. You are paying for it, and you have already paid certain nonrefundable fees. If the appraisal is out of line—and I have experienced this more than once—find out why the appraiser felt the value was lower than for comparable properties. Point out the positive attributes of your planned house, such as better windows, better construction, or a better heating system, if your plans call for it. Most appraisers do not know whether a cast-iron heating system is better than a steel-case system, but it is. If the appraiser will not back off and everyone involved thinks the appraisal is out of line, demand your money back (including the appraisal fee), and try another lender.

The appraiser must appraise the land and the structure separately to be able to determine a value for the entire property. The appraiser will also consider the highest and best use of the property according to the uses allowed by the local zoning code and the actual design of the building. If the zoning allows multifamily as well as single-family use, the property should be more valuable because of the potential for that additional use and for future income. However, although the property may be zoned for additional uses (see Chapter 4), the building design or floor plan must be able to accommodate the additional use without major renovation.

The appraisal will include a description of the property, a description of its location, and an explanation of the various uses allowed under the zoning code. Separate values are placed on income-producing property and on the land. The appraisal will specify a time limit for the marketability of the property on the basis of the current appraised value. Because real-estate markets change constantly, appraised values will change constantly as well.

If an appraiser based in a relatively expensive area is appraising a property in a less expensive area, he or she will tend to produce an appraised value higher than local appraisers would assign to the same property. Local appraisers are more familiar with local markets.

A typical appraisal includes the items listed in Figure 9.1.

Local appraisers are more familiar with local markets.

- The appraiser's qualifications
- Information on the general area
- A map of the area highlighting important attributes
- Information about the neighborhood
- A description of the scope of the appraisal
- An explanation of the purpose of the appraisal
- A definition of market value
- A description of the zoning that affects the property
- A copy of the zoning map
- A description of the property
- Plans or a sketch of the building(s)
- Pictures of the property and the surrounding area
- A copy of a flood-plain map (if the property is located within a flood plain)
- A map or survey of the subject property
- An explanation of the highest and best use of the subject property
- A description of the method of appraisal
- An explanation of the market, cost, and income approaches used to determine value
- A direct-sales approach to the area and the land
- Comparable maps or surveys attributed to land sales
- For income property, a vacancy, credit loss, and expense analysis

FIGURE 9.1 Appraisal criteria

Approaches to Appraisal

To derive the appraised value of your project, the appraiser will use at least three separate approaches: the market-data approach, the cost approach, and the income approach.

The *comparison* or *market-data approach*, which compares the subject property with other like properties, is usually the most popular method to establish fair market value. You will hear the real-estate broker mention *comps*, which is short for *comparables*. Comps are like (similar) properties that the broker and the appraiser use to establish the appraised value of the property. For example, if your planned home has three bedrooms and two bathrooms, the appraiser will look for comps with the same number of bedrooms and bathrooms that have sold in the same general area of the town or county. The appraiser will also use comps to determine the value of the building lot. If your target home has a family room, attached garage, or fireplace, the appraiser must find comps as close to your home as possible and make adjustments to the value to arrive at a fair market value for the property.

Another approach an appraiser will use is the *cost approach*. Using this approach, the appraiser calculates the current cost of reproducing the same (like) property. Most appraisers use the comparison approach and the cost approach when dealing with residential loans. They will ask real-estate brokers for comparables of other homes sold in the general area. Once the appraiser has established the value, the lender can determine the loan-to-value ratio, or the amount to lend against the appraised value. The appraiser must also consider the current market conditions. If the supply is high and demand is low, the appraiser may have to *cushion* the appraisal with a lower fair market value, in the understanding that market conditions may force home values down in the future and that the lender's mortgage may exceed the desired loan-to-value ratio.

A further way to establish value is the *income approach*, which is reserved for properties that either produce income or have the potential to produce income. The appraiser will require a breakdown of the existing or

You will hear the real-estate broker mention comps, which is short for comparables.

Most appraisers use the comparison approach and the cost approach when dealing with residential loans.

146

potential income and expenses as well as an explanation of how the space is to be used. Combining all the other information compiled and including a risk factor for loss of income or increase in taxes or insurance, the appraiser will determine the additional value for the use and income.

Leave Room for Error

When submitting your plans, materials list, and plot plan to the bank appraiser, add a small cushion to those numbers to give yourself a margin for error. If your package comes to $100,000, try to find a way to include an additional $10,000 for a total of $110,000. If you are as familiar with Murphy's Law as I am, you will probably experience more than one problem on the job that will require additional money. You don't want to placed in a position of sacrificing areas of your home to pay for a problem. However, you must be able to qualify for this additional money. You don't have to use the money; you simply want to know it is there as insurance. If you learn that you don't need it, don't borrow it. You will pay additional costs to borrow this cushion amount, but those are minimal compared to the potential of losing square footage, forgoing that fireplace, or using vinyl siding or stucco instead of stone.

Add a small cushion to those numbers to give yourself a margin for error.

Create the Financing Package

Your financing package will depend on your qualifying for a permanent mortgage. The package will be the construction loan, which may or may not include money for the lot purchase, and the commitment for the long-term permanent loan that will replace (pay off) the construction loan. With the entire package available, the lender can formulate your financing. Review Chapter 1 to refresh your memory on financing.

When you meet with your lender, present copies of the contractor bids, a copy of the land contract, and a copy of the general contractor agreement if there is one. If your experience in construction is limited, the lender

Think about it. If you were the lender, would you risk this kind of money on a venture in which the principal player doesn't know what he or she is doing?

may be hesitant to approve this form of loan. Think about it. If you were the lender, would you risk this kind of money on a venture in which the principal player doesn't know what he or she is doing?

This is where the general contractor or experienced contractor-helper comes in, and this is a major reason why you need written agreements. If you can show either that you have the needed experience or that you will have expert help to complete the project, the lender will feel much more confident in taking the risk to lend you the money.

That is exactly what I did when I started out in the building business. I didn't know much about construction, but I took on a partner who had more than 20 years' experience, and we were approved to build seven homes the first year. The lender will also (subconsciously) form an opinion of you on a personal level. Are you the type of person who can carry out this idea? Can the lender work with you if a problem comes up? Will you live up to your agreement to pay the interest on time and not abuse the availability of this much money? Banking is still a people business, and much depends on your ability to convince the lender that you can do what you say. You need to make the right impression. It helps to use a technique called "mirroring" that I recently learned at a seminar: When you meet with a banker, wear business attire. When you meet with the contractors, wear jeans and boots. Make them feel comfortable when they meet with you. When you mirror people, you make them feel more at ease.

If you qualify for the financing and the appraiser agrees that the completed project will substantiate the loan to value, you need to structure the financing to avoid excessive closing expenses. *Closing a loan* means paying all the required fees and executing (signing) all the required documents so the loan can be filed with the county clerk as a lien against the property. The lien protects the lender in the event of a default on your part. If the problem cannot be worked out, the lender has the right to foreclose on the lien, take possession of the property, either complete the project or not, and sell the assets to satisfy the debt. Any shortfall in money generated by this action will be charged to you, along with all legal fees and

Any shortfall in money generated by this action will be charged to you.

TABLE 9.1 Construction Draw Schedule

Lot acquisition (balance due)	$ 20,000
Permits and fees	$ 5,000
Upon completion of lot clearing, grading, installation of footing	$ 8,000
Upon completion of foundation, concrete slab, rough plumbing, and electric	$ 12,000
Upon completion of all framing and installation of all exterior windows and doors	$ 15,000
Upon completion of all insulation, Sheetrock, painting, and HVAC system work	$ 15,000
Upon completion of roofing, siding, exterior trim, and landscape	$ 8,000
Upon completion of final electric including all fixtures, final plumbing, interior trim including all interior doors, and kitchen and bath cabinets	$ 10,000
Upon completion of final grade, carpet, and interior tile, and submission of C of O	$ 7,000
Total draws	$100,000

penalties. Once the loan is closed, as each phase of construction is completed, you are entitled to *draw* (receive a portion of the funds) sufficient money, according to a preapproved schedule, to pay for all labor and materials.

Table 9.1 shows a typical draw schedule. It is simply a guide; your schedule may use percentages or actual dollar amounts. You should be able to draw any amounts required as long as you can prove that the work was completed.

The *Certificate of Occupancy* (C of O) is the final notice from the municipality that the project has been inspected and approved for occupancy. Find out from the building inspector's office in your target area how occupancy is authorized when the job is completed, and make sure you understand the procedure for inspections. I will cover the inspection process later in this book.

Find out from the building inspector's office in your target area how occupancy is authorized when the job is completed.

One Loan—One Closing

When I first ventured into the construction business in the early 1970s, banks were still in the more-is-better mode. If you didn't have deep pockets (which I didn't), and if you didn't have a track record with the lender (which I didn't), the lender looked on you as fresh meat on the table.

The construction lending process was divided into two parts. The first part was the approval for the permanent financing. The lender wanted to know that you would qualify for the entire amount upon completion of the project. I was charged an application fee, an origination fee equal to *one point* (1 percent) of the amount of the total loan. I was charged an additional one point of the loan for a commitment fee. The application fee was about $250, and the points added up to 2 percent of the loan amount. I was then handed a piece of paper stating that I was approved for the amount requested, subject to the required closing fees.

The second part of this orgy of greed was to apply for, pay the fees (again) for, and receive approval for the construction loan, which was about 80 percent of the permanent loan.

By this time I had paid two application fees, two points on the construction loan, and two points on the permanent loan. Add to these fees the closing fees for each loan for my attorney, the bank's attorney, and the title company's attorney; the recording fees; the transfer tax; the mortgage tax; the title insurance premium for each loan; the initial appraisal fee and the final appraisal fee; the costs of the check prints and final working drawings; and the before and after surveys, and lunch was a cup of hot chocolate.

Essentially, the lender was charging twice for the same money.

Essentially, the lender was charging twice for the same money. I would close on the construction loan first to be able to have the money to build the house. The construction loan was approved for one year, at a higher rate of interest than the permanent loan rate, and I was billed monthly on the amount borrowed. In those days, the lender would not finance the purchase of the land. Either you bought the lot or—like me—you became very creative with financing. When the project was completed, you went back to the lender and closed the permanent loan, which paid off the construction loan. Normally my homes were presold, or at least sold before the closing of the permanent loan, but I had to pay all of the advance fees anyway, essentially paying twice for the same money.

Lenders today are a little easier to deal with.

Lenders today are a little easier to deal with. You should package the construction loan and permanent loan in one closing. If you will be a one-time builder, the lender may charge you commitment fees or origination fees. That is why I suggest that you shop your needs with more than one lender. The mortgage business is highly competitive, and most fees are negotiable.

If a lender wants to charge fees, negotiate these fees as much as possible. If the commitment fee is equal to one point or 1 percent of a $100,000 loan, that 1 percent equals $1,000. If you can negotiate that fee to $1/2$ percent, you will save $500. It's worth a try.

The loan should be structured in a way that allows the permanent loan to take over automatically when the project is completed or after a specified time. Most construction loans are approved for at least one year and carry interest that is payable monthly, interest only.

The loan document may contain language indicating that the construction loan may be modified. It means that even though the original loan was based on a one-year term with interest-only payments, that agreement can be modified to change the payment terms to a long-term mortgage and an adjusted interest rate. This will avoid the double closing-cost exposure.

Certain lenders today will also finance up to 95 percent of the entire package, *including the lot purchase and the closing costs,* as long as you qualify for the loan. This means that you need only 5 percent of the entire package in cash to buy the land and build your dream home.

What Is a Mortgage?

You are probably eager to get out there and begin your search—but finish your homework first. The better you understand the process and the terminology, the easier it will be for you to complete your task successfully.

Let's understand what a mortgage is. A mortgage is a *pledge* to repay a loan using real estate as *collateral* for the loan. Collateral is something of value given as a pledge of security for a loan.

The borrower is called the *mortgagor* (also *obligor*), and the lender is called the *mortgagee* (also *obligee*.) The mortgage will be filed as a lien against the property. A *lien* is a hold or claim that one person has upon the real property of another. At the closing, you will sign a *mortgage note*, which signifies your responsibility to repay the amount borrowed. There will also be a *mortgage bond*, in

Certain lenders today will also finance up to 95 percent of the entire package.

151

TABLE 9.2 Six-Month Amortization Schedule

Payment number	Remaining principal	Monthly payment	Principal payment	Interest payment
1	$107,527.80	$789.93	$72.20	$717.33
2	$107,455.12	$789.93	$72.68	$716.85
3	$107,381.96	$789.93	$73.16	$716.37
4	$107,308.31	$789.93	$73.65	$715.88
5	$107,234.17	$789.93	$74.14	$715.39
6	$107,159.53	$789.93	$74.64	$714.89

which you promise to repay the loan on the terms agreed to in the mortgage note. You *amortize* the loan by repaying the principal amount of the loan over time. Refer to Table 9.2 to see how a mortgage amortizes. The unpaid principal gradually declines. The monthly payment remains the same, but the principal portion of that payment increases as the interest portion decreases. This is known as a *self-liquidating* or *declining-balance mortgage*.

Do not expect to remember all the terms mentioned in this book. This book is a reference guide. Take it with you throughout the process, and refer to it as the need arises. Refer to the index in the back to locate terms you will be exposed to. Do not be afraid to interrupt a conversation to look up the meaning of a word or phrase. Professional people just love to dazzle you with footwork and 10-dollar words. If you do not understand, ask for an explanation. If you do not receive a satisfying explanation, *you* explain that if you are not comfortable with the terminology and the process, you will go somewhere else.

To cover all the lending instruments and programs available would require another book. There are many types of mortgages available. The following sections describe the most popular ones. Your loan officer will explain the other forms of financing if necessary.

The most popular form of mortgage has been the fixed-rate mortgage.

Fixed-Rate Mortgage

The most popular form of mortgage has been the *fixed-rate mortgage*. The interest rate is fixed and will not change for the *life of the loan*. The monthly payment stays the same, although as time passes, the payments will include more of the principal and less of the interest, making the loan a declining-balance or self-liquidating mortgage (see Table 9.2). The standard amount for this type of loan has been a loan to value of up to 80 percent of the sale price or appraised value, *whichever is lower.* The lender will accept the appraised value over the sale price as the correct value for the property.

Adjustable-Rate Mortgage

An adjustable-rate mortgage (ARM) is just what the name implies. With the wild fluctuations of interest rates in the late 1970s, lenders realized that by holding fixed-rate mortgages over long periods, they subjected themselves to increases in the cost of money they themselves borrowed, or the amounts they had to pay their depositors on CDs and other instruments. The banks found themselves paying out more interest then they earned. The ARM was born in response to that problem.

With the ARM, the lender sets the rate for the first year; the interest may rise or fall at preestablished intervals ranging from three months to five years, with the most popular ARM adjusting annually. The interval depends on which *index* the lender uses to establish the rate. The index could be the yield for one- to five-year Treasury securities. Ask the loan officer which index will be used for your mortgage, how the index performed in the past, and where you can obtain annual copies of the index. With an annually adjusted ARM, the rate adjusts on the *anniversary* of the loan (the day you closed on the loan). Ask about the amount of the *margin* used to calculate the interest for your loan. The margin is the amount that the lender adds to the *index rate* to arrive at the interest rate applied to your loan. The margin amount remains constant, but the index rate changes every year. If you know the margin amount, you can combine it with the index rate to arrive at the total adjusted rate.

If you do not plan to own the house for a long time, an ARM is more beneficial than a fixed-rate mortgage. The ARM will start out at a lower rate than the fixed-rate mortgage, with a cap on the annual increase. If you expect to own the house for only a few years, you will save by paying less interest in the early years, as opposed

If you do not plan to own the house for a long time, an ARM is more beneficial than a fixed-rate mortgage.

153

TABLE 9.3 Actual Percentage Rate When Discount Points Are Charged

Int. rate	1 Point	1.5 Points	2 Points	2.5 Points	3 Points
5%	5.09%	5.13%	5.18%	5.22%	5.27%
5.5%	5.59%	5.64%	5.68%	5.73%	5.78%
6%	6.09%	6.14%	6.19%	6.24%	6.29%
6.5%	6.6%	6.65%	6.7%	6.75%	6.8%
7%	7.1%	7.15%	7.2%	7.25%	7.3%
7.5%	7.6%	7.66%	7.71%	7.76%	7.81%
8%	8.11%	8.16%	8.21%	8.27%	8.32%
8.5%	8.61%	8.67%	8.72%	8.78%	8.83%
9%	9.11%	9.17%	9.23%	9.29%	9.34%
9.5%	9.62%	9.68%	9.73%	9.79%	9.86%
10%	10.12%	10.18%	10.24%	10.3%	10.37%
10.5%	10.62%	10.69%	10.75%	10.81%	10.88%
11%	11.13%	11.19%	11.26%	11.32%	11.39%
11.5%	11.63%	11.17%	11.76%	11.83%	11.9%
12%	12.13%	12.2%	12.27%	12.34%	12.41%

to paying the higher fixed rate from the beginning. Remember that the average owner today remains in the home between three and seven years. If you are unsure which type of mortgage is best, ask the lender for a print-out of an annual percentage rate (APR) schedule (see Table 9.3)—which shows the actual interest rate charged for both the ARM and the fixed-rate mortgage—and estimate how long you plan to stay in the home. In any case, most of the monthly payment for both kinds of mortgages goes to interest in the early years.

What Is APR?

The term that should concern you more than points or interest is annual percentage rate (APR).

The term that should concern you more than points or interest is *annual percentage rate (APR)*. APR is the actual rate of interest you will pay, which may not be the rate advertised if points (discount points) are involved. If points are charged, the lender must add that prepaid interest to the amount of total interest quoted to show the *actual APR* of the loan.

For example, if the loan amount is $100,000, the annual interest charged is 7⁵/₈ percent (7.625 percent) payable over 30 years, and the lender is charging 2¹/₂ points, the actual APR will be 7.89 percent, not 7.625

154

percent. Table 9.3 shows how to calculate the APR when discount points are charged. Ask the loan officer to tell you the APR is as well as the interest rate.

Be courteous when you make your appointments, and show up on time. Loan officers usually work on a commission basis. Volume of business is important, and their time will be short. Be courteous; you are relying on the loan officer to find you the best possible deal for your mortgage.

Obtain as much information over the phone as you can. Certain lenders will refuse to give you any information unless you go to their offices, where they have a chance to sell you something. If you are simply shopping around, explain that, and you will not need to dig out your old tax records. If you have narrowed your choice down, the loan officer will ask for supporting information at the first meeting. Find out beforehand whether the lender requires an *advance-application fee.* An application fee is *not* normally refundable, and sad to say, there are those who will take your money gladly whether you receive financing or not. Most successful agencies do not require advance fees. They will be happy to accept your fee when *you* have decided to accept *their* services, after you have been *prequalified.*

In Table 9.3, in the column heads, you see that the number of points charged ranges from one to three. In the far left column, you see numbers from 5 to 12 that represent the interest rate. In the remaining columns, you see the annual percentage rate (APR), or the actual interest charged when points are paid.

Let's look at an example. In the far left column (interest rate), move down to the first number (5). The interest rate is 5 percent. Now slide to the right, to the first number (5.09 percent). Look above that number, and you will see "1 point." If the interest rate quoted was 5 percent and the lender is charging one point, the actual interest charged (APR) is 5.09 percent. Even though you pay the points in cash in advance or finance them as part of your settlement costs, by law the lender must calculate those points into the overall interest costs of the loan to show quoted interest plus points to equal total interest charged, or APR. The APR will change with the interest rate, the points charged, and the length of the mortgage.

They will be happy to accept your fee when you have decided to accept their services, after you have been prequalified.

155

Before you commit to a transaction, find out the APR for your loan.

Before you commit to a transaction, find out the APR for your loan to verify that you are not paying too much overall interest.

Loan Cap

An adjustable-rate mortgage places a *cap* on the amount by which the interest can increase each year, with an overall cap over the life of the loan known as a *lifetime cap*. For example, let's say that your loan starts out at $4^{1}/_{2}$ percent-interest, with an *annual cap* of 2 percent of the original loan amount. That means the interest can rise to $6^{1}/_{2}$ percent after the first year and can rise again 2 percent each year thereafter. But don't panic. Most states have implemented *usury laws* that will allow lenders to increase interest only to a certain point. The present lifetime cap of your hypothetical ARM is 6 percent over the life of the loan, at 2 percent per year, for a maximum interest rate of $10^{1}/_{2}$ percent. At today's rates, $10^{1}/_{2}$ percent is expensive. However, consider that because the going rate is around 8 percent for a fixed-rate loan, the longer the economy allows lower rates, the more you will benefit by saving $2^{1}/_{2}$ percent in the early years of the loan. Even if the rate climbs to $6^{1}/_{2}$ percent next year, the fixed rates are also climbing, and you will still be better off. Also, during that time you will have had the tax benefits of ownership.

Another cap rate used is a *periodical rate* that will limit the rate increase from one adjustment period to the next. Suppose you have a periodical adjustment rate with an annual ARM (adjusted once per year) and your annual cap is 2 percent. If the index climbs to 4 percent, you will only be charged the maximum of 2 percent extra for that year. As the index fluctuates, adjustable rates can decrease as well as increase. However, if the index remains at 4 percent for the following year, your rate will adjust upward another 2 percent.

Convertible ARM

There is a way to allay your fears about the adjustable-rate mortgage. Certain ARMs, known as *convertible ARMs*, allow you to *lock the rate* to a fixed rate at a certain point if the rates start to climb. Check with the mortgage professionals to see what the current options are. The fixed-rate mortgage and the ARM are the two most common instruments used today. Remember that the lender will still qualify you at the *current fixed rate,* or at least 2 percent above the current ARM rate of interest, even though you are applying for an ARM.

Second Mortgage

If you are short on cash and long on income, you may be able persuade the owner of the property you wish to purchase to hold a *second mortgage (purchase-money mortgage)*. A second mortgage is also a lien on the property, and it enjoys the same rights as other mortgages. The second mortgage (also called a *secondary loan*) is just that: second in place behind a first mortgage.

The danger of a second mortgage is that, if you default on the first mortgage (in this case the construction loan) and the bank forecloses, the second mortgagee will not be guaranteed his or her money in full. The bank holding the first mortgage will be satisfied first. In the western states, any contractor liens will have to be negotiated, and what is left over can be paid to the holder of the second mortgage; in the East the second mortgagee has more power. Most sellers will not hold a second mortgage.

Foreclosure

To *foreclose* means to take away the right to redeem. In real-estate financing, if you do not live up to your obligation to repay the loan, the lender can proceed to foreclose your property.

When you mortgage a property, you agree to allow the mortgage note to be filed as a lien against the property. You sign a mortgage bond (also known as a *promissory note*), agreeing to repay the mortgage.

If you fail to live up to the agreements, you will be *in default* on the loan, and the lender will have the right to foreclose the lien against the property, take possession of the property, and resell it to recoup the investment.

Remember that the lender will still qualify you at the current fixed rate.

A second mortgage is also a lien on the property.

To foreclose means to take away the right to redeem.

157

First Mortgage

Any bank mortgage will be a first mortgage (primary loan).

Any bank mortgage will be a first mortgage (primary loan) unless the lender is financing another type of loan such as a home-equity *(secondary)* loan. The bank will always be *first* in the event you decide to seek financing from other private or public sources for additional money, using the house as *collateral.* Be careful if you do decide to obtain additional mortgages or liens against the property. *Most mortgages require immediate repayment in full of the entire balance due if additional financing is placed against the property without the written permission of the first mortgagee.*

Be careful if you do decide to obtain additional mortgages or liens against the property.

Balloon Mortgage

You will hear the term *balloon mortgage* or just *balloon.* For example, a mortgage may be written to be *amortized* on a 30-year schedule, but the principal balance remaining may balloon—*become due and payable* in the 15th year. A lender uses the balloon to limit the risk of a lengthy commitment and at the same time to make the loan affordable by allowing repayment on a longer amortization basis.

Bait and Switch

Advertising is designed to make you respond.

As you forge through the mortgage-rate jungle, you will see that rates do not vary substantially from one lender to another. However, you will see rates quoted at a very low level, almost too good to be true—and they probably are. Advertising is designed to make you respond. When you respond to an ad, you give someone the opportunity to entice you to buy. To get your attention, a lender or broker will advertise a *teaser rate* that is lower than most other rates. As with anything else in the world, there is no free ride in the finance business. Although the rate may be attractively low, *read the fine print.*

I recently read a teaser-rate ad placed by a local savings bank for a one-year ARM mortgage with an interest rate of 3.75 percent, an APR of 6.31 percent, and a 2-percent-per-year cap with a lifetime cap of 9.75

percent (we're getting good at this). The ad said, "No hidden fees." At the bottom of the ad I read:

> Upon completion of the 5th year of the balloon mortgage, customer has the option to refinance or pay off the existing balance. *Rates are scheduled to change weekly.* ARM rate may change after consummation. Annual percentage rate *includes points* and does not include PMI.

The ad stated, "No hidden fees," but the main body of the ad included no mention of how many points would be charged. I guess points are not considered a fee. Also, you just read in the quoted paragraph what a balloon mortgage does. The advertisement entices the customer to call about the attractive low rate, but to accept that rate is to accept a mortgage that will balloon—or require payment in full—in the fifth year of the loan. In addition, the rate is subject to increases of 2 percent per year up to 9.75 percent. Moreover, there are points calculated into the loan, but the ad does not say how many points you must pay to obtain that attractively low rate. Also, the rates will change *weekly*—what a deal!

I call this type of advertising *bait and switch*. The leader entices you to call and stop into its loan office by advertising the low rate. Once a representative explains the terms and cost of the loan, you will be presented with many other financing packages the bank offers, and then they GOTCHA.

Don't be offended. You will see this bait-and-switch tactic used often throughout your journey to home ownership. It's all part of the game.

Shared-Equity Mortgage

A mortgage that may interest you if you are a first-time buyer short on cash is the *shared-equity mortgage (SEM)*. A blood relative can loan you the money you need to accomplish the purchase. You agree that he or she will share in the *buildup of equity* in the property for a fixed number of years. In the future, you will refinance or sell and pay back your relative's principal amount plus his or her *share of the equity.*

A lender or broker will advertise a teaser rate that is lower than most other rates.

A blood relative can loan you the money you need to accomplish the purchase.

Bridge Loan

A bridge loan is not a mortgage; rather, it's a personal loan.

One more important type of loan is a *bridge loan*. A bridge loan is not a mortgage; rather, it's a *personal loan*. Let's say that you are transferred to a new area. You find the home you like, but you are short on cash for a deposit or down payment because most of your assets exist as equity in your existing home, which has not yet closed title. If you do not currently own a home, you may have something else of value, such as stocks or bonds, that can be posted as collateral. Using the equity in these assets, you may obtain a bridge loan from the lender you are using for the new house to *bridge the gap* until your existing home is sold.

Prepayment Penalties

Why would a bank penalize me if I paid its money back?

A common practice lenders use to make the loan comfortable for you is to refrain from charging you a penalty (this practice may change in the future) if you decide to pay the loan off early. Why would a bank penalize me if I paid its money back? Lenders commit funds for specific periods at specific rates of return on their investments. It is common today for most lenders to sell mortgages off to the *secondary mortgage market*. The secondary mortgage market consists of an organization of investors sponsored by the federal government called *Freddie Mac* (the Federal Home Loan Mortgage Corporation), whose stock is owned by the thrift industry. The mortgages are packaged and resold as securities on the stock market. Another federally sponsored organization is *Fannie Mae* (the Federal National Mortgage Association), which provides funds to primary lenders and guarantees securities backed by a portion of its mortgage portfolio. Your lender makes its profit by collecting fees and points at the beginning of the transaction and earns a maintenance fee for continuing to service the loan.

Make sure that your mortgage has no prepayment penalty clause.

If you opt in the future to repay your loan before it is due, you may be penalized for this prepayment because the lender has sold off the loan, and the investors who bought it expect a certain rate of return. *Make sure that your mortgage has no prepayment penalty clause.*

Borrower's Responsibility

You, the borrower, are completely responsible to the lender to ensure that the money drawn for construction is used only for construction. In certain states, state law

TABLE 9.4 Construction Cost Schedule (Materials and Labor)

Date	Bid price	Invoice	Check date	Check no.	Amount paid
Professional fees					
Lender fees					
Lot clearing, stumping, and grading					
Excavation					
Footings, foundation/slab					
Plumbing (including rough and finish)					
Well/water, septic/sewer					
Framing (including exterior doors and windows)					
Roofing and siding					
Insulation and Sheetrock					
Electrical (including rough and finish)					
Paint and trim (including bath and kitchen cabinets)					
Carpet and tile					
Finish grading and landscape					
Painting and staining					
Miscellaneous expenses (cleaning)					

To avoid mixing your building funds with your personal funds, establish a separate checking account.

Make a schedule of your own.

requires that any funds drawn for the purpose of building a home must be used only to build that home and for no other purpose.

To avoid mixing your building funds with your personal funds, establish a separate checking account for the purposes of building this house. You can give the account any name, such as "XYZ Builders." An appropriate name will also show contractors and suppliers that you are serious and a potential source of income. If you wish, you can file a Doing Business As (DBA) form with the county clerk's office (you are John Smith, doing business as XYZ Builders).

Make sure that you account for all monies spent. Create a spreadsheet like the one shown in Table 9.4.

Make a schedule of your own. Leave enough room within each category to record four to five payments. This way you can keep track of the costs and see how they match up with the original bid prices. If there is any discrepancy about who paid whom for which job, you will have a record of each payment, reflecting the date and amount paid, the recipient of the check, and the check number.

CHAPTER
10

The Construction Process

Stay on Schedule!

Time is money in the construction business. Contractors are paid for the time they invest in each project. If a job is delayed, a smart contractor will have several other jobs under way to fill in the day and make a living. That is the main reason contractors overbook their time. Your house is merely one project; the contractor needs many projects to make a living. If you are delayed, expect to lose that contractor for at least several days.

Anticipate at least three weeks' delay in the overall construction schedule due to delays in material deliveries or contractors' commitments to other projects.

Time is money in the construction business.

Stake the Building Lot

Staking the building lot should take about one to two days.

If you are new to the building business and don't normally work with tools, let those with experience do the on-site work. One crucial preparatory step is physically locating the proposed house, driveway, and water and sewer lines on the lot before the actual construction begins. This entails *staking* the corners of these proposed improvements. Figure 10.1 illustrates a simple example of staking.

Let those with experience do the on-site work.

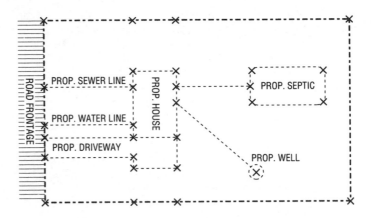

FIGURE 10.1 Staked lot

Your surveyor will take accurate measurements and install the survey stakes.

Your surveyor will take accurate measurements and install the survey stakes. In Figure 10.1, you can see the approximate locations of the house, the driveway, the water/well and sewer/septic lines, and the well. The *X* at each corner of each proposed improvement marks the area where a *survey stake* should be placed. Also note that survey stakes are placed at the corners of the building lot and also on the property line on each side at the *setback* where the house foundation is to be located. There are also stakes at the corners of the septic system, along the water and sewer lines, and generally anyplace on the lot where improvements will be constructed.

By staking the entire improvement area, you are drawing a picture—similar to a follow-the-dots drawing—that shows the locations and sizes of the features of your proposed construction. To improve on the stakes, buy a bag of white chalk at the hardware store. For each separate improvement area, tie a string to a corner stake, then string the stakes from one to the next until you have connected all of the stakes for that area. Draw a white chalk line by walking along the string and shaking the chalk onto it. When you are finished, you will see your foundation, garage, water/well, septic/sewer, and driveway drawn onto the lot. The markings will show the contractors where to start and where each improvement will be built.

The setback requirements set forth in a zoning ordinance (see Chapter 4) are the minimum distances required from the property line to the perimeter of the house. Figure 10.2 shows how the setback requirements affect the building lot. There are individual setback requirements for the front yard, the side yards, the rear yard, any accessory buildings (such as a detached garage), and the septic system.

Make sure your house will fit on the lot after the required setbacks have been accounted for. For example, if your house is to be 40 feet wide and your building lot is 75 feet wide at the *main building line,* you would subtract 40 from 75 to arrive at a balance of 35 feet. The main building line is the location of the front of the foundation (facing the street) after the front-yard setback is calculated. The zoning ordinance will dictate how wide the lot must be at the main building line to accommodate your house. At the main building line, you must allow for the width of the house and the required side-yard setbacks. Returning to the example, if you divide 35 feet in half, you will have equal measurements of 17$1/2$ feet. If you center your house on the 75-foot-wide lot, you will have 17$1/2$ feet left over on each side. If the zoning ordinance requires 20-foot side-yard setbacks, your house will not fit on the lot. You will have to reduce the size of your house, buy additional land to meet the setback requirement, turn the house sideways on the lot if that is allowed by the ordinance, or find another lot.

The setback requirements set forth in a zoning ordinance (see Chapter 4) are the minimum distances required from the property line.

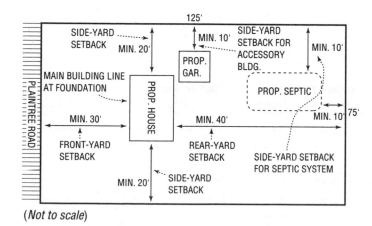

(*Not to scale*)

FIGURE 10.2 Example of setback requirements

If you can prove that compliance with the zoning ordinance would constitute a hardship, you may file for a variance with the zoning board or zoning officer.

If you can prove that compliance with the zoning ordinance would constitute a hardship, you may file for a *variance* with the zoning board or zoning officer. If most of the homes in your area were built before the adoption of the zoning ordinance and their setbacks are less than 20 feet now required, the zoning board should grant you a variance. Most zoning boards will not grant variances on the basis of economic hardship; they don't care whether you make money or not.

If the building lot needs a variance, be sure to make your purchase of the lot subject to the granting of the needed variance. You don't want to be obligated to buy a lot that you can't use.

Order Materials

Order all materials in advance. One way to avoid confusion when ordering materials is to use *purchase orders* and *change orders*. Table 10.1 shows a typical purchase order.

Call your suppliers at least two weeks in advance of the relevant points on your construction schedule to guarantee delivery of the materials you need. Call again one week in advance to make sure the materials are at

TABLE 10.1 Purchase Order

Purchase order

Order no.	Job no.
Date ordered	Salesperson
Deliver to	Phone

Requested by		**Driver Truck No.**	**Del. terms**	
Date	Quantity	Product description	Unit price	Total
				Subtotal
				Tax
				Total

TABLE 10.2 Change Order Form

Change order no.		*Job no.*	
Date of change		Salesperson	
Location		Job phone	
Date	Product description	Unit price	Total
Replaced by			
		Original price	
		Discount	
		New price	
		Subtotal	
Supplier approval		Date	
Job super approval			

the warehouse. If they are not, you may have to locate materials somewhere else. You can't afford to lose contractors at the start of the game. This would set a bad precedent and undermine your credibility. Have needed materials delivered to the site a day in advance to allow the contractors to start work early each day. If you make a change in materials, whether due to unavailability of the materials originally ordered or to a simple change in style, use a change order form. Table 10.2 shows a simple preprinted change order form.

Excavation and Foundation Work

Foundation, water/well, and sewer/septic work should take about three to five days.

After the surveyor and engineer complete their measurements and staking out, the first contractor to work on the job will be the excavator. He or she will determine the timing and the number of machines needed on the job. You would love to have everyone show up at once, but you shouldn't have too many workers on the job simultaneously. The workers would just get into one another's way, and the work would take longer.

The first contractor to work on the job will be the excavator.

169

The excavator can have one machine excavating the footings while another machine excavates the septic area and a third one digs the trenches for the water or electrical lines. The excavating contractor will decide how many machines will be needed at any time.

Verify with this contractor how long each job will take. You must allow for delivery of the materials the next contractor will need to start work. Most excavating contractors also install water, sewer, and septic systems. If this is the case, your contractor should be able to dig and install the water and sewer lines in one or two days. The septic, depending on the type of system, should take from one to three days. Coordinate the installation of the water and sewer with the inspections. The building inspector may be the one to approve the water and sewer lines; the county health department engineer may approve the well and septic systems. Make sure the appropriate inspectors are notified of the installations and will be on hand to approve them as soon as they are completed.

Figure 10.3 shows the various water levels in the ground. At the top of the illustration you see the ground surface. Just below the surface you see *soil water,* and then *suspended water.* Both of these water sources can be called *surface water.* Below the *suspended water* is the *capillary water,*

Make sure the appropriate inspectors are notified of the installations and will be on hand to approve them.

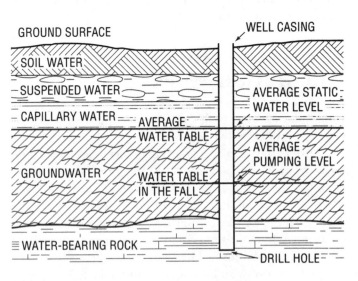

FIGURE 10.3 Various water levels for wells

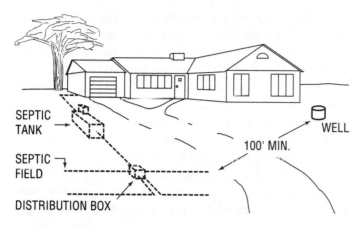

FIGURE 10.4   Example of a simple septic system

or the area where the two adjoining layers of water inter-act. Below the capillary-water level is *groundwater.* Notice the two levels of the *water table:* the average water table and an adjusted level for fall, when water levels are nor-mally lower. Below the groundwater level is the *water-bearing rock,* with crevices and fissures to allow the ground-water to seep into the hole left by the drilled well. In some areas of the country, the rock may be much closer to the surface, or the water table itself may be much lower or even nonexistent.

There are many types and styles of septic systems. A septic system is simply a system in which waste is com-bined with air and water in a way that allows the waste to break down through the presence of natural bacteria. The treated *black water* (effluent) is allowed to flow through a system of pipes to be absorbed by the soil and evaporate into the air. Figure 10.4 illustrates a simple sep-tic system.

Table 10.3 shows New York's current requirements for septic tank size.

A septic system is simply a system in which waste is combined with air and water in a way that allows the waste to break down through the presence of natural bacteria.

TABLE 10.3   Minimum Septic Tank Size Requirements in New York

1, 2, or 3 bedrooms	1,000-gallon tank
4 bedrooms	1,250-gallon tank
5 bedrooms	1,500-gallon tank
6 bedrooms	1,750-gallon tank

171

The septic tank is installed near the house, within 10 to 15 feet of the foundation. The effluent (black water) is allowed to drain, by gravity, into the septic tank. Figure 10.5 illustrates a typical septic tank.

A septic tank can be built out of stone, brick, or concrete block.

A septic tank can be built out of stone, brick, or concrete block. Some older tanks were made of steel, but they eventually rusted away over the years. The newer tanks are either precast concrete or fiberglass and are now required by most local health departments.

The effluent flows from the house down the waste drains and into the septic tank, where the septic process begins to break down the solid waste. The solid waste is full of microorganisms such as bacteria. Without getting too technical, I like to describe the process as the good guys eating up the bad guys.

Most microorganisms are heterotrophic; this means they use organic material for both food and energy.

All microorganisms require the basic elements of carbon, nitrogen, phosphorus, and sulfur, as well as some trace elements. Microorganisms are small chemical factories in which raw materials are processed. Most microorganisms are *heterotrophic;* this means they use organic material for both food and energy. The biochemical process, in which microorganisms convert waste and use it as energy is known as *metabolism.* The process in which matter is broken down into simpler forms is known as *catabolism.* Bacteria produce organic catalysts, enzymes

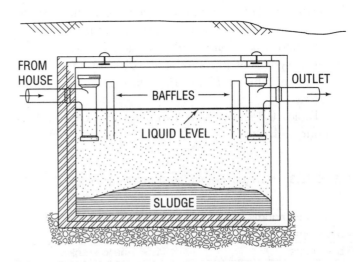

FIGURE 10.5 Example of a typical septic tank

that speed up metabolism. Eventually, a constant rate of growth is reached, and the cultures reach a death phase where the surviving organisms are fewer than in the previous generation. The dead organisms settle to the bottom of the tank as sludge. The constant inflow of new waste material allows the process to continue. Eventually the sludge will accumulate in the bottom of the tank, and the tank will have to be pumped out. Some experts recommend pumping the tank each year, but that poses the potential problem of removing the microorganisms that are needed for the septic process (the good guys).

Depending on how you use or abuse a septic system, you should be able to use the system for several years before you need to pump. Everything that goes into the septic tank must be biodegradable. If you are in the habit of simply flushing everything down the kitchen sink, you will have to break that habit. With a municipal system, people don't have to worry about what is flushed away, but with a septic system, you need to be more careful. You can't simply drain the cooking oil or the leftover pasta into the system. You can't pour in paint or solvents. It's common sense: Anything that will kill you if you drink it will kill the bacteria your system needs to function. Similarly, if you drink cooking oil, it will clog *your* system, and it will do the same to the septic system.

Although most health departments require that the clothes washer empty into the septic tank, I do not agree. Soap, unless specifically designed as a biodegradable product, does not break down; it forms a film inside the pipes. The soap builds up into a thick scum, plugging the tank, and the tank will have to be pumped.

Contact the local health department for literature about the operation of septic systems. That information will contain good advice on what should and should not go into the system and will save you aggravation and money in the long run.

I favor installation of a dry well for the disposal of shower and washer water. A dry well is simply a hole dug down about 4 to 5 feet and filled with rocks or gravel. The shower and washer water (gray water) drains into it and eventually into the soil. Many areas do not allow dry wells because of the potential to pollute the surface water and eventually the groundwater.

It's common sense: Anything that will kill you if you drink it will kill the bacteria your system needs to function.

173

The excavating contractor will leave a backhoe on the job to work with the plumber. The plumber will have to install the sewer line and any drain lines you may want installed through or under the footings before the slab is poured.

If you applied the information in Chapter 4 regarding lot elevation and drainage, you have purchased a lot on which the location for the house is higher than the surrounding ground.

The depth of the excavation for the foundation depends on the style of the home you are building.

The depth of the excavation for the foundation depends on the style of the home you are building. There are basically three styles of foundation construction, with various materials used. Figure 10.6 is a simple illustration of the three styles: slab, crawl space, and full foundation. The prevailing type of foundation in the eastern states is either the crawl space or the full foundation. In the West, the slab-up style is customary.

The *slab* or *slab-up* style of foundation entails minimal excavation because you are pouring a concrete slab at ground level. With the *crawl-space* style, you elevate the house slightly and build under it a space (the crawl space) that gives you access to the plumbing and extra storage. The floor can be either dirt or a poured slab. The *full foundation* or full basement is set in the ground deep enough to allow at least a 7-foot, 6-inch ceiling height from the concrete floor to the floor joists or the bottom of the first floor. At least 1 to 2 feet of the foundation should be above grade to allow for the installation of basement windows or vents. The floor of the full foundation will generally maintain the temperature of the surrounding ground, 55 degrees, to a depth of at least 6 feet. In the hot summer months, condensation forms on the cool

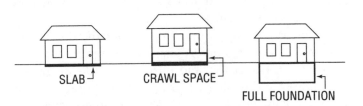

FIGURE 10.6 Slab, crawl space, and full foundation

floor and walls; that is why basements smell musty. Adequate ventilation can prevent the build-up of mold.

Following is a simple formula for calculating how much concrete you will use:

> 1 square foot of concrete 4 inches thick = 576 cubic inches
>
> 1 cubic yard = 27 cubic feet = 46,656 cubic inches
>
> 46,656 cubic inches divided by 576 cubic inches = 81 square feet of coverage.

To calculate the yardage required, simply divide the square footage by 81.

Use this formula to calculate all of your concrete needs. For example, for the 4-inch slab for the floor of a 1,500-square-foot home, 1,500 square feet divided by 81 equals 18.52 square yards of concrete. Add 5 percent to 10 percent for a waste factor, and you will need to order about 20 yards of concrete for a 1,500-square-foot slab that will be 4 inches thick.

If the walls of the foundation are to be poured concrete and you will pour the walls 8 inches thick, you simply double the formula. Multiply the length by the width of the wall, and double the amount needed to accommodate the required 8 inches of thickness. You could also divide the number 81 by 2 to equal 40.5 (because you are doubling the formula) and use that number to derive the same yardage. I prefer to use 81 as the constant number and not confuse myself any more than is necessary.

Footings

Excavating the footings takes about one to two days.

It is very important to build the right size footings. The entire house with its tremendous weight will sit on the footings. You must design the footings to accommodate the soil conditions and the thickness of the foundation wall.

The best way to determine your soil conditions is to dig holes in various areas of the lot to a depth matching that of your proposed foundation. If you are building slab-up, you only need to dig down 3 to 4 feet. If you propose a full foundation, you will need to dig down at

Adequate ventilation can prevent the build-up of mold.

It is very important to build the right size footings.

175

least 10 to 12 feet. As you dig down, you will see layers of various types of soil, as illustrated in Figure 10.7. These layers tell you what type of footing you will need. If soil tests have been conducted on the site as part of the engineering for the subdivision, locate the engineer who performed the tests to obtain a copy of the results; you may not have to pay for your own tests. In areas of predominately slab-up construction, mostly in the western states, the soil type will be less variable than in the East, and your engineer should have a record of the area's soil types.

As you dig down, you will first see the topsoil, possibly a layer of gravel and clay mixed with rocks and stones. Under that you might find hard clay, and farther down you may find good gravel soil or rock or a high water table or any mix of these conditions.

If you hit rock, you will stop there.

If you hit rock, you will stop there. You will either spend the money to blast or raise the house to accommodate the rock. If you hit water, you should likewise raise the foundation level to accommodate the water. You need to dig down to *suitable bearing ground*, dense soil that has been undisturbed and is of a composition that will support the weight of your house.

The design of your footings must allow for the soil type and the size and depth of the foundation. If the soil is clay, which can be spongy, you must install a footing that will be wider and possibly higher than the usual.

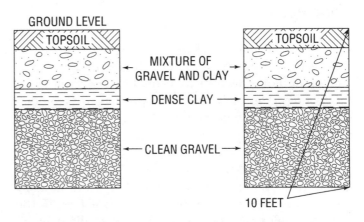

FIGURE 10.7 Soil types

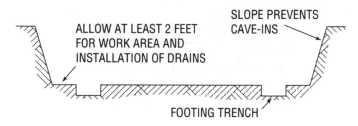

ALLOW AT LEAST 2 FEET
FOR WORK AREA AND
INSTALLATION OF DRAINS

SLOPE PREVENTS
CAVE-INS

FOOTING TRENCH

FIGURE 10.8 Side view of a footing trench

The wider or *spread footing* spreads the weight of the house over a larger area. I've installed spread footings over 2 feet wide and 2 feet high to allow for a very soft soil condition and experienced no problems. This type of footing is also called a *floating footing.* Figure 10.8 shows the side view of a typical footing.

You will dig and install footings for your foundation, front and rear steps, patios, porch stanchions, and any other structural feature that needs support in the ground. A typical footing will be sized to accommodate the size and type of your foundation wall. Most footings are at least 8 to 14 inches wide and at least 4 to 6 inches high. If you are building a full foundation, you should install a footing at least 14 inches wide. If you are using concrete block for the foundation, you will need 10-inch block in the ground (to be buried) and 8-inch block above ground. If you are installing a poured concrete foundation, allow for a *key* to be pressed into the concrete footing. Figure 10.9 illustrates a *footing key.* This key allows the poured

If you are installing a poured concrete foundation, allow for a key to be pressed into the concrete footing.

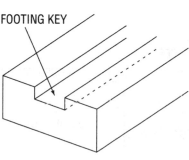

FOOTING KEY

FIGURE 10.9 Footing key

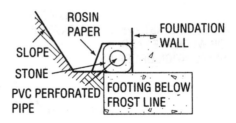

FIGURE 10.10   Footing drain

concrete for the wall to *marry* with the concrete footing, just as the pieces of a tongue-and-groove wood floor fit together.

In the eastern states, where rainfall is common and the ground may become saturated with water, you will need to install a *footing drain* (see Figure 10.10). This drain may be of a flexible plastic (PVC) tubing with *weep holes* throughout, or you can use rigid PVC septic pipe. The holes in the pipe allow water to seep into the pipe, which channels it away to a lower elevation. Your mason, excavation contractor, or plumber can install the footing drain. The pipe is installed at the level of or just on top of the footing. It is surrounded by gravel or 1¼-inch stone and then covered with rosin paper to prevent soil from silting into the pipe. Footing drains can be placed either on top of the footing or alongside it. Figure 10.10 shows a simple footing drain.

If you plan to add brick or stone to the exposed portion of the foundation, you need to incorporate a *brick shelf* or recess into the foundation to accommodate the weight of that material. Figure 10.11 illustrates a typical brick shelf.

Your mason, excavation contractor, or plumber can install the footing drain.

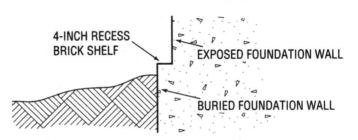

FIGURE 10.11   Brick shelf

If you plan to install brick on the exterior of the house, you can use the following simple formula to calculate how many bricks you will need. Count on about *7 bricks to cover 1 square foot,* allowing for about 5 percent waste. At 7 bricks per square foot, you would use 700 bricks to cover 100 square feet of the exterior. Measure the height and width of the area you will cover. Multiply these numbers to calculate the square footage, and multiply again by 7 to calculate the number of bricks you will need to cover that area. For example, let's say that you have measured the front of your house and you want to use brick to face an area that measures 8 feet high and 20 feet wide. Multiply 8 by 20 to get 160 square feet. Multiply 160 square feet by 7 bricks per square foot. You will find that you need at least 1,120 bricks to cover the proposed area.

Measure the height and width of the area you will cover.

If your house location is not on level ground, you may have to install a *stepped footing* to allow your foundation to remain level. A stepped footing does just what the name implies: It steps up or down to accommodate the changing elevation of the lot. Figure 10.12 offers a simple illustration of a stepped footing.

Pouring the footings and/or foundation takes one day. Constructing a concrete-block foundation will take from two to five days, depending on the depth and size.

You may have to install a stepped footing to allow your foundation to remain level.

Combination Foundation and Slab

In the western states, where slab-up construction is the norm, a combined concrete slab and foundation may be

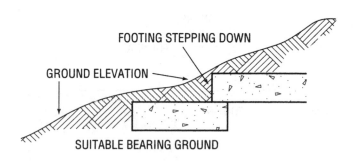

FIGURE 10.12 Stepped footing

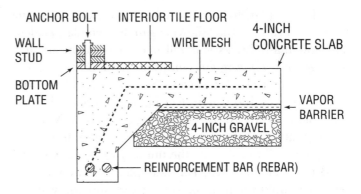

FIGURE 10.13 Combination foundation and slab

poured at the same time. Figure 10.13 shows a simple side view of a combination slab and foundation section.

In the eastern states, where full foundations are more common, you would build a 10-inch-block wall for the buried portion of the foundation and use 8-inch block for the exposed portion. The foundation is built from the footing up, with enough room allowed for installation of the footing drains on the outside and the concrete slab on the inside. Figure 10.14 shows a side view of a typical footing, footing drain, foundation wall, and concrete slab with a vapor barrier and a gravel base.

The mason will even out the ground where the slab is to be poured.

The mason will even out the ground where the slab is to be poured, then will install at least 4 inches of gravel or washed stone evenly to form the floor. If possible, this stone or gravel should be compacted mechanically to prevent settling. The vapor barrier (consisting of plastic

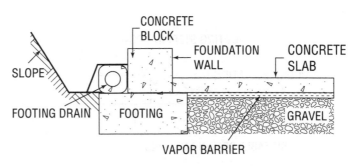

FIGURE 10.14 Foundation, footing, slab

sheets) is installed over the gravel, and the 4-inch concrete slab is poured over the plastic.

The mason will *waterproof* the outside of the buried portion of the foundation wall with hot tar or bituminous asphalt. Where the foundation is exposed, you can use a masonry parging to seal the concrete or block. This idea is to make the foundation as secure as possible against water infiltration.

Make sure that the area near the foundation is clear of large rocks that could be pushed back against the wall when the excavator *backfills* the area. After everything is installed—water lines, utility lines, sewer lines, power lines, whatever will extend through the foundation wall or up through the slab—the excavator will backfill the excavated material against the foundation to even out the ground. During periods of heavy rain, when the ground is saturated with moisture, there can be as much as 1,500 pounds of water pressure against your foundation wall. If there is as much as a pinhole, water will find it and enter the house. I have seen an excavator backfill large rocks directly against the foundation wall, where, if the rocks themselves do not damage the wall, they create pockets where water can accumulate against it.

Inspect the footings to make sure they are not cracked. Do the same for the wall and the slab. Make sure that the slab is level and flat and the walls are straight and plumb.

Concrete is full of water when it is poured, so it needs time to *cure,* to dry out gradually. It is a good idea occasionally to spray water onto the surface of the slab as it cures. This allows the concrete to dry evenly instead of from the outside in. Sometimes, when concrete dries too fast outside and the inside is still wet, cracks form. Some cracking due to settling is normal. The ground has been disturbed, and the gravel will settle as the weight of the concrete bears down on it. I call these normal cracks "spider cracks" because they look like portions of a spiderweb. If large cracks appear, you have a problem. You may have to remove and repour the slab, or you may be able to pour a new slab over the old one. The solution depends on what is causing the problem. If the weather forecast calls for rain or freezing temperatures, do not pour concrete or install block. You shouldn't pour con-

Inspect the footings to make sure they are not cracked.

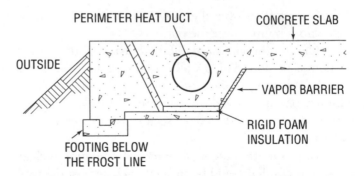

FIGURE 10.15 Cold-climate perimeter-heat foundation

crete unless the temperature will be at least 50 degrees or above for most of the day. If you are building in the winter months, you may have to cover the slab with plastic and install propane heaters to keep the concrete warm overnight.

Inspect all of the concrete joints between the sections of all of the walls to make sure there is no daylight showing through. You want the foundation to be sealed from the outside elements.

Inspect all of the concrete joints between the sections of all of the walls to make sure there is no daylight showing through.

If you are building a slab-up foundation in a cold climate, you may have to install heating ducts under the concrete slab. Figure 10.15 shows the side view of a foundation prepared for the installation of *perimeter heating.*

Framing

Framing should take from five days to one week, depending on the size of the home.

You are using good subcontractors; why use inferior materials? The lumberyard may try to sell you material that has been sitting out in the weather and is mostly warped pieces of wood riddled with knotholes. First, find another lumberyard where customers are treated with respect. Next, try to find lumber that has been *kiln dried.* Kiln drying is a slow drying process in which the moisture in the material is allowed to evaporate under low heat and warping is prevented as the wood dries naturally.

It has been my experience that *Douglas fir* is the best material to use for framing. The price difference between

THE CONSTRUCTION PROCESS

Douglas fir and other types is nominal. For your wall and roof sheathing, I recommend plywood of either grade C or grade D. Plywood is graded by the number of defects evident in the wood. You don't need to spend extra money on better plywood that will be covered by siding and roofing.

The most popular style of framing is known as *platform framing.* A typical platform-framed wall would look like the illustration in Figure 10.16. Framing a house is a little like building a sandwich. From the foundation wall, you install a Styrofoam insulating sill sealer. Over the sill sealer, you bolt the sole plate into place by using the anchor bolts in the foundation. You install the interior floor joists by nailing joist hangers to the header and nailing the floor joists to the joist hangers. You are basically building a large box that is attached to the sill plate. You install the subfloor over the floor joists and the sole plate over the subfloor. Nail the wall studs in place to the sole plate and top them with the top plates, and you have a wall system. Let-in cross bracing is installed where the studs are notched out to allow the brace to fit flush into the wall.

The most popular style of framing is known as platform framing.

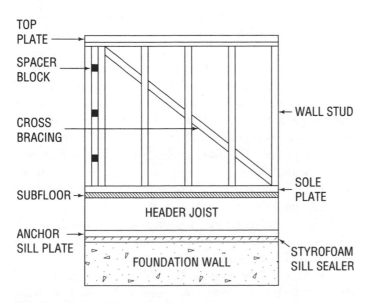

FIGURE 10.16   Platform-style framing

If you plan to install fiberglass tubs and showers, you must install them before closing in the walls. These units are in one piece, and they will not fit in after the walls are completed.

Check each room as it goes up to ensure that it is the right size, and check the size and placement of each window and door.

Check each room as it goes up to ensure that it is the right size, and check the size and placement of each window and door. If changes are needed, try to make them as the house goes up. Your subcontractor may charge a fee to make the changes, but he or she will surely charge a fat fee to change something after the structure is completed.

Consult with the plumber, electrician, and siding contractor as the framing goes up. Make sure that they know the house is being framed. If they need any accommodations, now is the time to make them, not later when the framer is on another job.

Make sure that you are using CDX plywood or better for your subfloor. This plywood should have an APA-approved stamp on the outside to guarantee its quality. The *C* and *D* refer to the various grades of the exterior of the plywood, and the *X* refers to the inside grade. This type of plywood will stand up to weathering and wetness better than the *particle board* favored by most builders. Particle board will *delaminate* (come apart) when it gets wet much faster than plywood will.

If you are installing ceramic or vinyl tile over a wooden subfloor, install a high-quality clear 1/4-inch plywood as the subfloor over the CDX to allow the tile to be glued down without pockets of air forming under the tile.

The local building codes may require corner bracing.

The local building codes may require corner bracing. This can be done with pieces of plywood nailed to each opposing corner to marry the corners together. You should use stud-grade wall studs to avoid warped and cracked pieces. The interior walls will be finished with Sheetrock. If you don't want your interior walls to be wavy, the studs must line up, and they cannot be damaged or warped.

You will continue framing to the roof, where, depending on the style of your home, you will use either standard framing lumber or trusses. You may also use trusses for the floor systems. Trusses are preengineered and premanufactured systems for walls and roofs that come

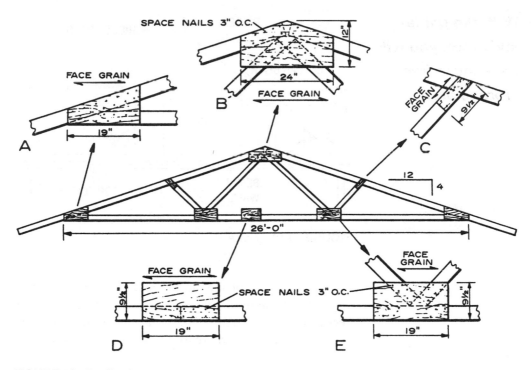

FIGURE 10.17 Roof truss

stacked on a truck. They are simply lifted into place and nailed. Figure 10.17 illustrates a typical roof truss.

The truss roof provides an easy way to frame the roof, but the supports within the truss preclude using the attic space for storage. The trusses must be framed either 16 inches or 24 inches on center, depending on the pitch of the roof. If you want to use the attic space for storage, you will have to frame the roof using conventional framing lumber to look something like the gable style shown in Figure 10.18. With the gable-style roof, even though you need support studs on the interior to hold up the roof, you will have more free storage area.

You will cover the roof rafters with plywood sheathing. Roofing paper covers the plywood, and the roofing material covers the roofing paper. The plywood not only provides the base to which the roofing will be attached, but it also spreads the weight of accumulated snow or of heavy roofing material, such as the masonry tiles used in the western states.

The truss roof provides an easy way to frame the roof, but the supports within the truss preclude using the attic space for storage.

With the gable-style roof, you will have more free storage area.

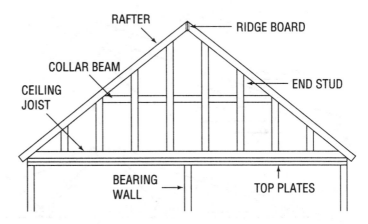

FIGURE 10.18   Gable roof

For a review of the most popular roof styles see Figure 3.8 in Chapter 3. Almost all homes are traditionally rectangular in design, with squared corners in every room. The roof is where you can set the style for the home.

If you are building in the western states, you may see a building section on your plans that resembles the illustration in Figure 10.19 provided by a new friend in

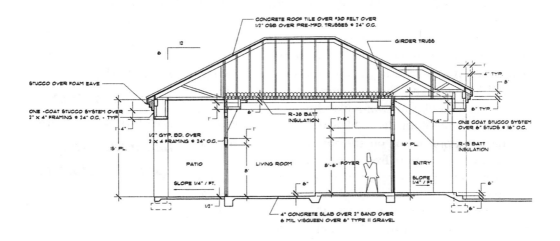

BUILDING SECTION A

FIGURE 10.19   Side view of western-style house

THE CONSTRUCTION PROCESS

Las Vegas, architect Gregory J. Moore. Notice the notes relating to stucco over the 2-inch-by-4-inch framing and the roof notes calling for concrete roofing tiles over felt over $1/2$-inch OSB over prefabricated trusses. Most of the construction in the West is slab-up, with no basements or crawl spaces.

Review your plans with your engineer or architect. Make sure you understand what the process is and how the materials are to be used. You need not be on site every day, and you do not need to know where everything goes or how it is installed. You simply need to have someone on site who does know these things *working for you*.

CHAPTER
11

Job and Draw Checklists

Stay within Budget

From the start of the building process, you need to keep track of your costs. The best way to keep the job costs in front of you is to use a budget control sheet like the example in Table 11.1. As the invoices come in, you can keep a running balance of the total costs to match against the overall budget you created by consulting with the engineer and using the contractor bids.

You can see that there are two or three blank lines in each category. These spaces allow for the stages in the payment schedule you may have agreed to with each contractor. It is a good idea to make two of these sheets: one to record the invoices as they come in and one to record the payments as they go out. Note the shaded lines to highlight subtotals. If you keep a running balance at the bottom of the sheet and match the subtotals with the original bid prices, you should be able to stay in control and not run short of money. These budget sheets will also help you coordinate your draws from the lender.

Another way to stay in control is to create a purchase order control sheet. When each purchase order is issued, place a copy in a special file and enter the purchase order information on a control sheet like the one illustrated in Table 11.2.

From the start of the building process, you need to keep track of your costs.

Another way to stay in control is to create a purchase order control sheet.

TABLE 11.1 Budget Control Sheet

Description	Material	Labor	Equipment	Subs	Bid price	Totals
Excavation						
				Subtotal		
Concrete						
Mason						
				Subtotal		
Plumbing						
Plumber						
				Subtotal		
Lumber						
Framer						
				Subtotal		
Windows						
Doors						
				Subtotal		
Roofing						
Roofer						
				Subtotal		
Siding						
Sider						
				Subtotal		
Electrical						
Electrician						
				Subtotal		

TABLE 11.1 *continued*

Description	Material	Labor	Equipment	Subs	Bid price	Totals
Insulation						
Insulator						
			Subtotal			
Sheetrock						
Sheetrocker						
			Subtotal			
Tile						
Tiler						
			Subtotal			
Paint						
Painter						
			Subtotal			
Trim						
Trimmer						
			Subtotal			
Carpet						
Carpet installer						
			Subtotal			
Plantings						
Landscaper						
			Subtotal			
Helper						
			Running balance			

TABLE 11.2 Purchase Order Control Sheet

P.O./No.	Date	Material	Vendor	Delivered	Amt. due	Date pd.	Ck. no.	Amt.	Total pd.

Construction Draws

The lender will issue you a commitment letter stating that you have been approved for a loan and specifying the loan amount. Accompanying the commitment letter will be a statement of a condition of the loan allowing for construction draws. (Review Table 9.1 in Chapter 9, an example of a draw schedule.) The lender may offer the draws in phases, such as a draw to pay for the land, another to pay for the excavation, another to pay for the foundation, and so on. Always try to stay a little ahead of the lender in the draw schedule. Refer to the budget you submitted to the lender. If the schedule offered to you is too restrictive, don't be afraid to approach the lender and ask that the draws be changed. Everyone wants your project to succeed. If the draws do not provide enough money to continue to pay the subcontractors and material vendors on time, the job will not be completed on time, you will pay added interest on the construction money because of the delay, and the vendors and contractors will charge you more money for the additional time. Construction delays are very expensive and are the reason many projects fail.

Everyone wants your project to succeed.

194

Match the Contractor Payments with the Draw Schedule

Review the lender's draw schedule with your contractors. Make them understand that you will be paid by the lender within so many days after completion of *their* work. If they do not adhere to the project schedule, you will not be able to draw the money needed to pay them. The lender may pay for partially completed work on a job that must be done in several phases, such as framing or plumbing. Partial payment for insulation or Sheetrock installation is less likely because these jobs should only take a few days each to complete. Likewise, the septic system or water and sewer lines should only take a few days to complete. If the excavator does not finish the work because the machine is on another job, make clear that payment will not be issued until each phase is completed.

Use the budget control sheet to track the overall progress of your project. You will see which contractors work hard to complete their respective jobs and which contractors you have to monitor constantly to make sure they get the work done.

Keep All Delivery Tickets for All Materials

Open a separate file to keep track of all delivered materials. As materials are delivered, the truck driver will have a delivery ticket that must be signed by someone on the job. If you have engaged a project manager, that person will sign for all deliveries. If you do not have a project manager, designate someone on the job to accept all deliveries when you are not there.

Review each delivery ticket for accuracy in the quantity and kind of material delivered, and physically inspect each delivery. If possible, count every piece to make sure you are not paying for materials that were not delivered. Ask the contractors to set aside any materials that are defective or damaged when delivered. You are

Open a separate file to keep track of all delivered materials.

entitled to credit for those materials, and the supplier should send someone to pick them up without charge. You may have to prove that an item was damaged before or during delivery. Your project manager or designated contractor will have to inspect each delivery to ensure that you will not be charged for damaged goods. A tactic that material suppliers use to surprise you is placing damaged goods in the center of a delivery, with the good material on the outside. Lumber companies are notorious for doing this. You must inspect every piece and save the damaged pieces for return and credit.

You must inspect every piece and save the damaged pieces for return and credit.

Do-Later Jobs

When you keep a running balance on the budget control sheet, you will see how the job progresses and how your finances are being used. Be careful about asking the contractors to do custom projects. Time is money in the construction business, and any side jobs you request will require additional funds. You will have to pay for the added materials and labor, and if there are too many side jobs, the costs may become prohibitive.

TABLE 11.3   Do-Later Jobs

- Outside gas grill or barbecue (install gas line in advance)
- Heated spa or swimming pool (install water lines in advance)
- Wooden decks or concrete patios (allow sufficient space)
- Skylights in roof (frame out interior of rooms and attic)
- Extra sliding or French doors (frame out interior of wall)
- Fireplaces and chimneys (frame out, pour chimney slab)
- Built-in microwave (frame out area or install cabinet and wire)
- Sidewalks and paved driveways
- Wet bars (install wiring and plumbing)
- Interior wall coverings and moldings
- Garage door openers
- Additional kitchen cabinets and counters
- Additional wall windows (frame out interior of wall)
- Electronic security systems and intercoms (install wiring)
- Sunrooms or patio covers (leave sufficient space)

If you want a contractor to do an extra job, use a purchase order control sheet. The control sheets allow you to keep your financial plan outlined and up to date at all times. Ask the contractor whether the extra job can be done later in the project schedule. If it can wait until later, you will have a better understanding of your overall costs and can decide then whether you can afford the extra expense.

You need to maintain a cushion of money for unforeseen events such as strikes, inclement weather, shortages, late deliveries, accidents, and price increases. We have all driven by projects that started out as someone's dream only to remain incomplete due to shortage of funds. Items that can be added later, after the house is substantially completed, are listed in Table 11.3.

Do-It-Yourself Jobs

There are many jobs that you can do yourself to save money and time on the project. Check with the local building inspector's office to ensure that a licensed contractor will not be needed.

You shouldn't need a license or experience to perform any of the jobs listed in Table 11.4.

All other jobs you should leave to the experts; that is what you hired them for. Try to be as helpful to the contractors as you can without becoming a pest. Let them complete their work, and buy them a beer when they're finished.

The control sheets allow you to keep your financial plan outlined and up to date at all times.

You need to maintain a cushion of money for unforeseen events such as strikes, inclement weather, shortages, late deliveries, accidents, and price increases.

There are many jobs that you can do yourself to save money and time on the project.

TABLE 11.4 Jobs to Do Yourself

- Cleaning up after each phase of construction to maintain a neat and safe site
- Painting and wallpapering
- Landscaping, planting your own, raking, and seeding
- Installing the mailbox
- Installing light fixtures (a license might be needed)
- Piling rocks to one side to use later in landscaping
- Cutting trees and shrubs to clear the lot and use later in the fireplace
- Organizing materials to be returned for credit

The Inspectors

You will need to get acquainted with five inspectors:

- The building inspector
- The bank inspector
- The insurance inspector
- The health department inspector
- The electrical inspector

If you begin your relationship with each inspector on a friendly and cooperative basis, you shouldn't have too many problems with each inspection.

You must ask yourself whether winning the argument will be worth the delay.

If you begin your relationship with each inspector on a friendly and cooperative basis, you shouldn't have too many problems with each inspection. I say "too many" because most inspectors have their personal idiosyncrasies, and they want certain things done that are not required by the building codes. If the job is not expensive or time-consuming, do it and get your inspection approval. If the job requires a lot of work and money, try to negotiate with the inspector. Bring your contractors and your engineer into the problem to convince the inspector that the demand is unreasonable. If you cannot resolve the problem any other way, you may have to appear before the town or city council to prove your point, but this may result in a long delay in the project. You must ask yourself whether winning the argument will be worth the delay.

Here's a case in point from my experience. I was developing a six-lot subdivision that fronted on a county highway. I had to build a new road about 1,000 feet into the site, and all of the lots would have access to my new road. When I applied for building permits for the two lots that fronted on the county highway, the building inspector, who doubled as the zoning officer, stated that the town zoning ordinance required any building lot fronting on a county highway to maintain a front-yard setback of at least 75 feet. The front-yard setback for frontage on a town road was only 50 feet. My new road was intended to be completed and dedicated to the town.

The zoning officer wanted me to meet the 75-foot setback requirement. To do so would have taken an additional 25 feet from my buildable area, which in turn would have meant that I could not build the houses to the size that I needed, which would have meant that two of my six lots would allow only smaller homes, which would have meant that one-third of my subdivision would not conform to the zoning ordinance, which would have meant that the entire subdivision would be worth less than I originally intended, which meant that I had to change this person's mind if I did not want to lose my shirt.

I reread the zoning ordinance regarding the requirements for ingress and egress to and from a building lot. The ordinance stated that the *front* of a lot was located where the main ingress (the driveway from the street) was located. That meant that my *front-yard setback* was *at the front of the lot*, which was *the location of the driveway*, which had *access from the future town road*, which required only a 50-foot setback instead of the 75-foot setback the zoning officer wanted. The zoning officer still maintained that because these two lots also fronted on the county highway and because the new road had not yet been accepted by the town, I still had to follow the 75-foot rule.

I took the argument to the town attorney, and she ruled in my favor. I did not make a friend that day.

Was my problem over? No! The zoning officer was also a member of the town planning board, and at the next meeting he convinced the board to change the zoning ordinance to require that *any* lot fronting on a county highway maintain a 75-foot setback. The law was passed immediately, and I again had to come before the zoning officer with an appeal for a variance to the new zoning ordinance to allow a 50-foot setback (now a side-yard setback), as called for in the previous ordinance. The zoning officer, embarrassed by the town attorney's decision in my favor, still argued with me that the variance would not be granted. I reminded the board that my subdivision had been approved by the town; it had been filed with the county before the zoning change and was therefore grandfathered. The 50-foot setback was the rule at the time of approval, and the board could not change the rules in the middle of my subdivision without a fight.

I took the argument to the town attorney, and she ruled in my favor. I did not make a friend that day.

The zoning board agreed with me and ruled in my favor. I was right, but I made an enemy of that building inspector, who dogged my project looking for problems until I sold all of the lots.

The Building Inspector

If you followed my recommendation, when you applied for the building permit, you sat down with the building inspector.

If you followed my recommendation, when you applied for the building permit, you sat down with the building inspector and found out what he or she would approve and not approve. As the house goes up, the building inspector will be on site to inspect the construction phases listed in Table 11.5.

You can see from the steps listed in the table that you will have someone else looking out for you as the job progresses and understand why it makes good sense to befriend the inspector if you can.

The Bank Inspector

The bank will hire someone to visit the site during each phase of construction to verify that the bills you are submitting for payment are real and that the materials and labor are really going into the job. The bank simply wants to know that when it pays for a foundation, the

The bank simply wants to know that when it pays for a foundation, the foundation will in fact be there when a representative comes to inspect it.

TABLE 11.5   Building Inspector's Checklist

- Footing trench before concrete is poured
- Foundation before framing is begun
- Water and sewer lines before and after pipe is installed
- Well trench and septic system before and after installation
- Framing as the house goes up
- Ceiling joists, roof rafters, roofing application
- Subfloors
- Insulation installation
- Plumbing, rough under, rough-in, and finished
- Siding application
- Sheetrock installation
- Finished lot grade
- Landscaping

foundation will in fact be there when a representative comes to inspect it.

The Insurance Inspector

The insurance company that issued your builder's risk insurance may have an inspector visit the site periodically to check for hazardous situations. You want to keep the job site clean and orderly. A sloppy-looking site reflects poorly on everyone, and a neat site is conducive to everyone's doing better work.

You will have to post "no trespassing" signs and rope off any holes in the ground. Flammable materials such as paint or gasoline for generators must be stored in fireproof areas. Don't let piles of nails accumulate or let loose boards lie about where someone can trip on them. The insurance inspector will point out areas of concern to the insurance company, and you will appreciate this attention. You don't want to lose your new house to fire or have someone injured because of carelessness if the mishap could have been prevented.

You will have to post "no trespassing" signs and rope off any holes in the ground.

The Health Department Inspector

Whenever you install a septic system or water or sewer lines, the state or county health department will be involved in approving the design and installation of these systems.

The inspector will visit the site to observe the *perc* (percolation) test for the septic system if it is not already approved. This official will review the design for the well and septic systems as well as the placement and depth of the water and sewer lines and will finally inspect the installation of each utility before you are allowed to cover them up. You made friends with the building inspector; try to do the same with the health department inspector. These people have the authority to make your life miserable if they want to nitpick. Review your plans with them before installation, ask if there is any work they need performed in addition to the approved plans, and be present when they are on the site to answer questions and assure them that the work will be completed properly.

You made friends with the building inspector; try to do the same with the health department inspector.

201

The Electrical Inspector

The local power company will hire an underwriting company to insure the installation of your home's electrical components. This work should be done by a licensed electrician. The underwriting company will send an inspector to verify that the wiring has been installed according to state and federal guidelines at the rough-in stage, before the insulation is installed, and again after the Sheetrock is installed. A final inspection will take place when the job is completed and all of the wall outlet covers are installed. If everything is satisfactory, the inspector will leave an approval sticker on the electrical panel box or in a window. *You cannot obtain your final certificate of occupancy from the building inspector without the electrical underwriter's final approval.* The underwriters can be difficult to track down at the last minute. Do not wait until the final days to call for an inspection. Arrange it well in advance of the mortgage closing, and make sure your electrician has everything completed. If your house does not pass the final inspection, you will not close the mortgage nor live in the house until the electrical inspector approves it.

Do not wait until the final days to call for an inspection.

Preparing
to Complete
and Close

Get It Done

When you began building your dream home, your adrenaline was pumping and excitement was at an all-time high. You then settled down into a routine, labor-intensive schedule of monitoring deliveries, collecting invoices, paying bills, and documenting the progress of the project. I have no doubt that by now you have learned at least several important lessons about the new-construction business. You may be thoroughly disgusted with the entire idea—exhausted and glad it is almost over—or you may be delighted with what you've learned and contemplating building more homes in the future. However you may feel, one thing is clear: The project must be completed on time to meet your personal goals and the lender's time limit for funding your permanent loan.

At this point you should be in your third month of construction and very close to completion. Your contractors may be starting to not show up on time or not show at all for several days at a stretch. You have the material on site, but the excavator has the equipment tied up on another job and can't complete your final grading for several days. The electrician has the same problem, and the plumber echoes the electrician. The mason also is busy on another job and can't come to pour the front steps and the sidewalk.

I have no doubt that by now you have learned at least several important lessons about the new-construction business.

205

In Chapter 11, I advised matching the contractor's payments with the lender's draw schedule to ensure that funds would be available for the contractors only if they completed all phases of their respective jobs. Now you may be sitting with an incomplete project and contractors who are not cooperating. They know that they have to complete their jobs on your site, but to them those jobs are money in the bank. They can begin other jobs on other sites, earning more money, and let you sit for a few days. You call them, screaming or begging them to come back; they explain that these new jobs were promised months ago, that they just had to go, and that they will return to your site within a few days. Unfortunately, a few days can easily turn into a few weeks if inclement weather intervenes.

Review Chapter 8 regarding the portion of the contractor's agreement requiring that the job be completed within a specified time. I hope you haven't forgotten to hold back at least 10 percent of the contractor's pay for each phase of the job.

Inform the contractors that you understand their predicament but that you must finish your project on time or risk losing the financing. If they cannot complete their jobs according to the contract terms, not only do they risk losing the 10-percent holdback, but they will also be responsible for any charges over the original prices if you must hire other contractors to complete the work at higher cost. Also, if through the contractors' actions you lose your financing, you will hold them liable to pay the difference in interest rates, if any, and any additional fees the lender charges to reapprove the financing. Additionally, you will charge them a full share of the carrying costs for the property such as taxes, insurance, and bank interest as long as the job remains incomplete and delays your closing.

When all of those costs are calculated, the contractors should be more amenable to meeting your needs.

Avoid Arguments

If you have a problem with a contractor and you have hired a project manager or designated one contractor to coordinate the project, ask that person to meet with you

Unfortunately, a few days can easily turn into a few weeks if inclement weather intervenes.

and the problem contractor to see if the difficulty can be worked out. The project manager speaks the same language as the contractor and may understand the problem better than you can.

If the problem is shoddy workmanship, refer again to Chapter 8 regarding mechanic's liens. In the eastern states, you can simply fire the contractor. In the West, you would do better to pay the contractor what is considered owed and file suit in civil court to retrieve your money. Document the problem by asking other experts to sign an affidavit that the work was not done properly. Take photographs of the shoddy work for the judge to see. A picture is worth a thousand words.

If the contractor does not show up on time and tardiness is a chronic problem, you can prove the tardiness by producing his or her invoices and payment record to show the contractor or a judge that your complaint is justified.

If the problem is simply bad chemistry between you and a contractor, you must decide whether a confrontation is warranted. If the contractor is doing a good job, is punctual, and is not overcharging you, I recommend that you limit your exposure to this contractor and get the job done. If the contractor is causing the problem by acting in a manner that affects the progress of the job, you may have to prove your point by asking witnesses to sign an affidavit documenting the problem and confront the contractor with the possibility of dismissal.

I had a contractor who loved to talk. Many contractors talk throughout the job to break the monotony, and as long as they keep working, I don't mind. This contractor, however, talked all day to the point where he interfered with the progress of other workers. He not only talked about himself but invented stories about other people. He was a true purveyor of gossip, and he gossiped over the two-by-fours instead of the back fence.

His work was passable—not perfect but acceptable. I had received complaints from some of the workers about this man's constant jabbering, and I finally confronted him, asking him to just do the work and not bother the others. He apologized, and I thought everything would be all right until, a few days later, I received another complaint from another worker. The contractor

The project manager speaks the same language as the contractor and may understand the problem better than you can.

Many contractors talk throughout the job to break the monotony, and as long as they keep working, I don't mind.

was again gossiping, but now there was a new twist. He was not only gossiping about other people, he was gossiping about me. He was inventing stories about my personal life (about which he had no knowledge) and creating an uncomfortable feeling on the project.

I confronted the problem contractor again and asked that he stop the gossip. He replied that his talking was his personal business and that as long as he did his job I should mind my own business. Wrong! I advised him that I thought my project would be better off without him, paid him what he was owed to that point, and sent him on his way.

There's more to the story. I heard several days later that another general contractor had also fired this man for the same reason. In the subsequent months, several more of his customers decided to do without his services. Sometimes, even if the contractor is doing a good job, it is better to hire someone different.

If the project is slowed down, do not set appointments with any of the inspectors until you are certain that the work will be completed and ready to inspect.

Communicate with the Inspectors

If the project is slowed down, do not set appointments with any of the inspectors until you are certain that the work will be completed and ready to inspect. There is nothing an inspector dislikes more than having to visit a project repeatedly to inspect the same job only to find that the job is not ready. Notify the inspectors of any delay, and promise to contact them when the job is ready for inspection.

Communicate with the Lender

The lender needs to know if the job is delayed.

The lender needs to know if the job is delayed. You have received a letter of commitment saying that the lender will close a permanent loan with you within a certain time frame. That money has been placed out of circulation and earmarked to be used for you. If you anticipate a long delay (of several weeks), tell the lender and ask if the loan commitment might be extended.

Many lenders, if it appears that a builder will not be able to deliver the job on time (this is not unusual), will offer to extend the commitment for funds until the job can be completed. There may be an extension fee to change the paperwork, but it's better than not getting the money at all.

Communicate with Your Attorney

If you have hired an attorney to represent you, keep him or her updated on the progress of the job. Your attorney needs to know of any contractor problems or delays that will require a new mortgage commitment.

If you have hired an attorney to represent you, keep him or her updated on the progress of the job.

If the seller of your lot is holding a subordinated mortgage, advise that party of any delays as soon as you can. I'm sure that the seller is looking forward to the money at closing and may even have a vacation planned. Give reassurance that you are in control despite the delay in closing. Be honest, and ask the seller to be patient.

Share with Your Loved Ones

If you are married or have a significant other in your life, you probably have not spent much time with that person. In this era of two working partners, there is already a shortage of personal time in daily life. And you want to cuddle while building a house? Forget it!

There is simply too much to do. You are holding down a full-time job and trying to supervise construction at the same time. You are visiting the suppliers and dealing with the banks and inspectors. Even if you have a project manager, there is a lot of extra work you must do. Who is paying the bills and arranging the bank draws? Who is picking out the colors and arranging the deliveries? Who is inspecting each delivery, and who is dealing with the contractors?

Who is paying the bills and arranging the bank draws?

Do yourself a favor: At least once a week, take your loved one(s) out to dinner and a movie. Forget the house for a while. A great time to visit the site together is late in the day, after everyone has gone home, or early in the

Do yourself a favor: At least once a week, take your loved one(s) out to dinner and a movie.

This is a good time to become part of the project in a more personal way.

morning before the workers show up. I used to love to walk through a house during each phase of construction and visualize what it would look like when finished. I would fantasize about my buyer's family playing in those rooms and on the front lawn or visualize just the couple sitting in front of the fireplace on a cold winter evening. This is a good time to become part of the project in a more personal way. This is your house. You (both of you) dreamed it, designed it, fought for and over it—and it is becoming a reality. Enjoy this adventure as much as you can. If problems arise, look and act upon them as challenges to overcome. The goal is to complete your dream house. Don't let anything or anyone deter you from reaching that goal.

Use a Precompletion Punch List

Even though your new home is almost finished, many items will still need to be completed before you can close with the lender and pay the final contractor bills. The list in Table 12.1 will guide you through areas that need to be inspected and alert you to items that need to be completed.

TABLE 12.1   Precompletion Punch List

Completed?		Items	Ready?	Notes
Yes	No			
☐	☐	Final grade	Ready for seed	
☐	☐	Landscaping	Plants	
☐	☐	Exterior siding	No gaps or holes	
☐	☐	Exterior trim	Painted	
☐	☐	Roof	No gaps/flashing	
☐	☐	Soffits	Painted/stuccoed	
☐	☐	Chimney	Flashing done	
☐	☐	Gutters/leaders	Installed	
☐	☐	Interior paint	No touch-up	
☐	☐	Interior trim	No touch-up	
☐	☐	Carpet	Tight seams	

TABLE 12.1 *continued*

☐	☐	Vinyl floor	No loose tiles
☐	☐	Ceramic floor	No loose tiles
☐	☐	Hardwood floors	Sealed/level
☐	☐	Ceramic baths	No loose tiles
☐	☐	Ceramic kitchen	No gaps in grout
☐	☐	Lighting	All working
☐	☐	Switches/outlets	All working
☐	☐	Fans	All working
☐	☐	Appliances	All working
☐	☐	Kitchen cabinets	Level, even
☐	☐	Bath cabinets	Level/to wall
☐	☐	Kitchen countertops	Level/matching
☐	☐	Bath countertops	Level/secured
☐	☐	Heating systems	Working
☐	☐	Cooling systems	Working
☐	☐	Faucets	No leaks
☐	☐	Sinks	No leaks
☐	☐	Laundry hookups	Working
☐	☐	Garage/finished	No touch-up
☐	☐	Concrete floors	No holes/gouges
☐	☐	Drains	Working
☐	☐	Windows	Working
☐	☐	Doors/locks	Installed/keys available
☐	☐	Decks	Level/not loose
☐	☐	Pools	No leaks
☐	☐	Equipment	Working
☐	☐	All keys	Accounted for
☐	☐	Electricity	On

Get the Certificate of Occupancy

I cannot count the number of times I have had to run around on the last day (the day of or the day before closing) making sure every item was completed before the building inspector showed up. Don't wait until the last day! Make sure everything the inspectors will need to

Don't wait until the last day!

211

approve is completed as far in advance of the projected closing date as possible. If there is a problem (and there always is), you will have time to correct it.

By now, the house should be almost completed, with the exception of a few small details that need to be addressed, such as paint touch-up or loose trim. You need to ask the building inspector for a final inspection. That inspection may vary from one area to another, but the basics for living in the house must be in place. The heating and cooling systems must be operational. At least one toilet must be secured to the floor. The kitchen range must be operational. The water and sewer systems must be operational. All electrical outlets, switches, and light fixtures must be installed, covered, and operational. If you have a bare wire in a closet where the electrician forgot to install a light, install a porcelain fixture with a bare bulb instead. The kitchen and bathroom floors must be covered with something. The exterior of the house will require some type of covering, possibly just tar paper, depending upon the inspector. The roof must be installed without leaks.

The electrical inspector will also walk through to ensure that all electrical systems are installed properly and are operational. The building inspector cannot release the certificate of occupancy until the electrical inspector approves the house. You will need to submit the required documents to the proper people (see Table 12.2) in order to obtain the C of O and close the transaction. You will also need the final "as built" plot plan from your engineer showing the house, garage, driveway, well and septic systems, topographical elevations, and lot lines. This final plot plan must be certified with your engineer's official stamp and personal signature to the municipality, the title company, the bank, and you.

You will also need certifications from the well and septic installers regarding the location, design, installation, and completion of those systems. The electrician and plumber may have to sign and certify that their installations were completed according to the original designs.

The same requirements may apply to the house. You may have to submit a final "as built" set of house

The building inspector cannot release the certificate of occupancy until the electrical inspector approves the house.

212

TABLE 12.2 Document Submission List

Final "as built" plot plan and final "as built" house plans	Building inspector
	Highway superintendent
	Water/sewer superintendent
	Title company
	Lender
	You
Certificate of occupancy	Building inspector
	Title company
	Lender
	Insurance company
	You
Insurance certificate	Lender
	Title company
	You
Certification of paid invoices and release of liens collected	Building inspector
	Title company
	Lender
	You
Copies of inspection reports	Building inspector
	Lender
	Title company
	Insurance company
	You
Results of laboratory coliform test on well water	Building inspector
	You

plans proving that the house was built according to the original plans.

If you have engaged a management company to pay the subcontractors, you will need certification from that company that all invoices have been paid and all releases collected. The company's final payout figures will need to coincide with the lender's payout figures. If you did not use a management company, you will need to provide verification to the title company and the lender that all bills have been paid and all releases have been signed and collected from the contractors. *All of this must be done and the documents submitted at least one week before the closing.* The lender will not schedule the closing without all documents submitted in advance.

If you did not use a management company, you will need to provide verification to the title company and the lender that all bills have been paid.

213

Make sure everything works before you pay all final bills.

Make sure the doorbell works and the toilets flush. Check the basement for leaks originating in the plumbing or coming through the foundation from outside. Check for gaps between the door and the door frame; do the same with all of the windows. Make sure *everything works* before you pay all final bills.

Test the oven, use the burners, and start the vent fan. Open the garage doors and inspect the garage interior in bright daylight. Check every window and door. Gently pull on the corners of the carpet to make sure it is tacked down. Check all kitchen cabinet doors to see if they are hung evenly and the hinges are tight. Check the seals around the showers, tubs, and sinks for leaks. Play with the thermostats for the heating and cooling systems. Have fuel delivered several weeks in advance to give the plumber a chance to run the heating system well in advance of any inspections.

Clean the house. Clean the kitchen. Have a drink—you're almost there.

The Final Day: What to Do Before, During, and After

Before the Closing

Congratulations—it's done! Close the final mortgage, and move in.

Walk through the house one last time a day or so before the final closing. Take the original punch list with you, and check off any small jobs that still need to be completed. If the contractor for a particular job has not returned to complete that job, feel free to hire anyone to complete it. You will need this final punch list to take to the closing. The lender will want to know what work still needs to be completed before writing the final checks.

Be careful: If any unfinished job(s) should entail an individual or combined completion cost of more than $500, the lender may hold back *three times* the estimated completion cost from your final payout. The lender does this to ensure that the work will be completed, knowing that you will not allow that much money to sit in the bank. In such a case, you will have to make sure that you have enough funds to finalize the closing without the holdback money.

If you use an attorney for your closing, make sure that he or she has copies of all certified documents needed to close the transaction. If you use an escrow

The lender will want to know what work still needs to be completed before writing the final checks.

217

company to organize the closing, the company must have all pertinent documents in advance of the closing date.

If the seller of your building lot is holding a second mortgage, make sure he or she is notified of the closing. The seller will have to provide you with a satisfaction-of-lien notice. The satisfaction will be recorded by the title company and paid by the lender.

This is it—the day you've been waiting for. You should be very excited, and I congratulate you. You have read this book, which is an accomplishment in itself, and you have learned a great deal about the real-estate business. You might even want to get into the business yourself some day.

But most of all, you have dreamed, and you've worked hard to make your dreams a reality.

You might even want to get into the business yourself some day.

During the Closing

Bring your entire file with you to the closing.

Bring your entire file with you to the closing. You should have your copy of the formal land contract and deed, the spec sheet or materials list, the working drawings and final "as built" plans, the original and final plot plans, copies of the verifications of invoices paid and releases from the contractors, your insurance policy, your punch list, and of course, your checkbook. It also helps to bring several photographs of the completed project. People become more involved in wrapping up the details when they see the what they are working for.

If an escrow company is handling the closing, you will simply go to the company office and sign all necessary documents. When everyone has signed all of the closing documents, and the title has been recorded (this should be done within a few days), it is yours—*just go home.*

In the eastern states, the closing is somewhat more complicated. Customarily, it takes place at the lender's office. At the table you will find your attorney (if you have one), the title company representative, and the lender's attorney. If the former owner has held a mortgage for you, his or her attorney may also be there. This is a very formal affair.

The bank will request (if it hasn't already) an original copy (not a photocopy) of your *homeowner's insurance policy* to verify that it is protected on the policy. If you do not already have a deed to the property, you will receive your actual title by deed. An example of a typical bargain and sale deed is illustrated in Figure 13.1.

The lender will give you a *settlement statement* (see Table 13.1), which shows any balances due for points, the

You will receive your actual title by deed.

BARGAIN AND SALE DEED

CONSULT YOUR LAWYER BEFORE SIGNING THIS INSTRUMENT—THIS INSTRUMENT USED BY LAWYERS ONLY

THIS INDENTURE, made the _____ day of, _____ nineteen hundred and

BETWEEN

Seller's Name and Address:

party of the first part, and

Purchaser's Name and Address:

party of the second part,

WITNESSETH, that the party of the first part, in consideration of Ten Dollars or other valuable consideration paid by the party of the second part, does hereby grant and release unto the party of the second part, their heirs or successors and assigns of the party of the second part forever,

ALL that certain plot, piece, or parcel of land with the buildings and improvements thereon erected, situate, lying and being in the (Town of Anywhere, State of Anywhere) and further described as (beginning at a stake at the corner of a property owned by whomever and wherever road, thence so many feet so many degrees so many minutes south to a stake, thence so many feet so many degrees so many minutes west to a stake, thence north so many feet, degrees and minutes, thence east so many feet, degrees and minutes, the point of the beginning). Being further described as: (Insert tax grid number and street address).

TOGETHER with all right, title and interest, if any, of the party of the first part in and to any streets and roads abutting the above described premises to the center lines thereof; **TOGETHER** with the appurtenances and all the estate and rights of the party of the first part in and to said premises **TO HAVE AND TO HOLD** the premises herein granted unto the party of the second part, the heirs or successors and assigns of the party of the second part forever.

AND the party of the first part covenants that the party of the first part has not done or suffered anything whereby the said premises has been encumbered in any way whatever, except as aforesaid.

AND the party of the first part, in compliance with Section 13 of the Lien Law, covenants that the party of the first part will receive this consideration for this conveyance and will hold the right to receive this consideration as a trust fund to be applied first for the purpose of paying the cost of the improvement and will apply the same first to the payment of the cost of the improvement before using part of the total for any other purpose. The word "party" shall be construed as if it read "parties" whenever the sense of this indenture so requires. **IN WITNESS WHEREOF,** the party of the first part has duly executed this deed the day and year first above written:

In Presence of:

FIGURE 13.1 Bargain and sale deed

TABLE 13.1 Lender Settlement Statement

Loan discount points (if not already paid)	$
Loan origination fee (if not already paid)	$
Credit report fee	$
Appraisal fee	$
Lender's inspection fee	$
Mortgage insurance application fee	$
Prorated interest (interest charged daily until principal payments begin)	$
Homeowner's insurance premium	$
Mortgage insurance premium (for PMI)	$
Property tax escrow	$
Mortgage recording fee	$
Mortgage tax (if any)	$
Lender's attorney fee (if any)	$
Lender's title policy premium (if required)	$

lender's attorney fee, and the appraisal. You will also sign a *title settlement statement* as illustrated in Table 13.2.

Your attorney will review the mortgage note (whose contents are outlined in Figure 13.2) and the mortgage bond (see Figure 13.3).

Other forms that you must sign include the *truth-in-lending disclosure for real-estate mortgage loans.* Information on this form includes the name and address of both borrower and lender, the annual percentage rate (APR), the total interest charged, the principal amount financed, and the total amount of principal and interest payments.

TABLE 13.2 Title Settlement Statement

Cash balance over financing	$
Title policy fee	$
Notary's or your attorney's fee	$
Recording fee for deed	$
Pest inspection fee (if not already paid)	$
Engineer's fee (if not already paid)	$
Certified survey fee	$
Adjustments with seller for fuel or other items	$
(Total these numbers and buy a lottery ticket ASAP) TOTALS	$

THE FINAL DAY

Mortgage Note

This document is considered a *security instrument* that describes the *borrower,* the *lender,* and the *property.* Also included are explanations and descriptions of the following topics:

A. *Borrower's transfer to lender of rights in the property* in the event of a default
B. *Legal description of the property*
C. *Borrower's right to mortgage the property and borrower's obligation to defend ownership of the property*
D. *Plain-language security agreement*
E. *Borrower's promise to pay*
F. *Monthly payments for taxes and insurance* (borrower's obligation)
G. *Application of borrower's payments,* used to pay the mortgage
H. *Borrower's obligation to pay charges, assessments, and claims* pertaining to water, sewer, and similar items
I. *Borrower's obligation to maintain hazard and property insurance*
J. *Borrower's obligation to occupy the property, maintain and protect the property, and fulfill any lease obligations*
K. *Lender's right to protect its rights in the property* in the event of a default on the loan
L. *Mortgage insurance*—promise to pay the premiums
M. *Lender's right to inspect the property* at reasonable times
N. *Agreements about condemnation of the property* (In the event of condemnation, you promise to use the condemnation award to pay off the lender first.)
O. *Continuation of borrower's obligations and lender's rights;* relates to assumption of the mortgage by another (In the event of an assumption when you sell, make sure that you are no longer signed on the mortgage and note.)
P. *Loan charges* (If the charges relating to this loan are considered unlawful, you are due a refund.)
Q. *Notices required under this security agreement* (If you change your address or there is a problem with the property, you are required to notify the lender by mail.)
R. *Law that governs this security agreement;* relates to federal and state laws incorporated into the agreement
S. *Borrower's copy* (You are entitled to copies of the note and mortgage.)
T. *Agreements about lender's rights if the property is sold or transferred* (The mortgage may be callable or payable in full if the property is sold.)
U. *Borrower's right to have lender's enforcement of this security instrument discontinued* (If the loan is paid on time and paid off, the lender must release you from this mortgage by filing a satisfaction of lien with the county clerk.)
V. *Note holder's right to sell the note or an interest in the note; borrower's right to notice of change of loan service* (You have the right to be notified in the event the lender sells the note, which is the norm these days.)
W. *Continuation of borrower's obligation to maintain and protect the property;* pertains to environmental laws, presence of flammable liquids, etc.
X. *Lender's rights if borrower fails to keep promises* (The lender has the right to call the loan and foreclose on the property.)
Y. *Lender's obligation to discharge this security agreement* (The lender must file the satisfaction when the lien is paid.)
Z. *Agreements regarding the state lien laws* (A rider may be attached to this agreement that further specifies the preceding details subject to state law.)

FIGURE 13.2 Mortgage note

Mortgage Bond

This form is your promise to repay the loan. It states the names of the borrower and lender, the property address, the principal amount borrowed, and the interest rate charged. The following topics are also included:

A. *Payments.* Designates the day the payments begin and the day they end.

B. *Borrower's right to prepay.* Specifies your right to make additional payments to reduce the principal amount any time without penalty; provides that the payments remain the same, with the interest adjusted to the reduced principal amount.

C. *Loan charges.* Sets forth the legality of the charges and specifies that any overcharges will be refunded to you.

D. *Borrower's failure to pay as required.* Defines the grace period allowed before you incur late charges and specifies the amount to be charged. States that your failure to pay the loan will be a default, sets the time limit for making up the payments, and states that if you default, the note holder has the right to call the entire debt as due and payable.

E. *No waiver by note holder.* States that even if the note holder does not require payment in full, he or she holds the right to do so at a later date.

F. *Giving notice.* Requires that any notices to you must be sent by first-class mail.

G. *Obligations of persons under this note.* Restates your obligations under the note and specifies that any others who may sign the note have the same obligations individually. If you have a cosigner to the note, each person is individually responsible for the terms of the note, whether one or the other pays the debts.

H. *Waivers.* Waives the rights of *presentment* and *dishonor.* Notice of presentment means that you waive your right to require that the note holder make demands for payment (he or she doesn't have to chase you). Notice of dishonor means that you have the right to require the note holder to give notice to any other persons obligated under this agreement.

I. *Uniform security code.* States that the note is a uniform instrument that may vary with jurisdictions and relates to the mortgage, deed of trust, or security deed that further describes the loan obligation. Further, explains the lender's rights if the property is sold or transferred (the lender may require payment in full).

FIGURE 13.3   Mortgage bond

The loan is broken down by the number and amount of the required payments.

You must also sign the *RESPA* form; this is a federal requirement. The Real Estate Settlement and Procedures Act (RESPA) requires the lender to have you acknowledge that you have been told how the closing process works and what all of the documentation means and does and further, that you fully understand your financial obligations regarding the mortgage. The loan is broken down by the number and amount of the required payments, and the beginning and ending dates of payment. The form states the type of loan—fixed rate or variable rate. It identifies how the loan is secured (by the property). It specifies how much can be assessed in late charges, whether prepayment of the loan will carry a penalty, and whether the loan is assumable.

You will also sign a *disclosure form* for the lender certifying that you have been informed about the actual percentage rate. The disclosure form sets forth the annual percentage rate (APR), states that the points are included in the overall rate, and it explains that the interest (including points and PMI) is calculated over the life of the loan.

Tired of signing yet? Another form is the *owner's estoppel certificate*, which certifies to the lender that the mortgage is a first mortgage and a first lien on the property. The property address, loan amount, loan payment schedule, and loan interest are stated. Reference is made to the mortgage and mortgage note.

One more form to sign is the *compliance agreement.* This is another promise by you to comply with all requests to furnish the lender any further information it may need regarding your mortgage application. You certify that all of the information provided on the application is true. You further (again) promise to abide by the terms of the mortgage and note.

This is another promise by you to comply with all requests.

Also, you will receive individual invoices from the title company for the title policy, the lender's attorney's fee, your attorney's fee, and your homeowner's insurance (if not already paid). The lender will probably require a tax-escrow account to ensure that property taxes are paid on time. You may be required to cover up to one year's taxes in advance.

In certain western states, if the property closes escrow through an escrow company, *you are not entitled to take possession of the house until the closing documents have been recorded in the county records (unless you already own it),* usually several days after the closing. Verify this matter with your broker and escrow company.

After the deed is recorded, it is sent back to your attorney or to you. And you're done. You have writer's cramp and you're broke, but you're happy.

Because most mortgages are written to begin the principal reduction 30 to 45 days after closing, there will be an adjustment for the interest charged on the mortgage from the date of closing to the date the mortgage

In addition, the lender will probably require that the homeowner's insurance be paid in full for at least the first year.

begins to amortize. In addition, the lender will probably require that the homeowner's insurance be paid in full for at least the first year.

The title attorney will hand you a bill for the title policy, and your attorney will hand you a bill for his or her services. Remember the hot dogs and beans.

If you have held back money from any contractor who has not completed a job and that contractor demands payment, *have one of the attorneys draw up an agreement that the work will be completed within a certain time and the money released when the job is completed. Sign it, and have the contractor sign it.* Make sure that you have collected all warranties for all equipment installed, including the well pump, appliances, heating and cooling systems, and any other products. If problems arise in the future, you will have no one to scream at but yourself. If there are new home warranties available, buy one just in case. The insurance is worth a few hundred dollars. For more information on warranties, write to the National Home Warranty Association, 498 Thorndale Drive #200, Buffalo Grove, IL 60089. If there are no other problems, you have the keys, you own a new home, you're broke, and you're smiling—only in America.

After the Closing

Go to your new home and congratulate yourself with a bottle of champagne.

Go to your new home and congratulate yourself with a bottle of champagne. Over the following days and weeks, make note of any problems you encounter. There is no such thing as a perfect house. Every new home must have the bugs worked out just as a new car does. The major problems are usually not with the construction itself but with the contractors' lack of interest in returning to make repairs. Once they are paid, they are gone. It is not unheard of to hold back 10 percent of the contractors' final payments for 30 days after completion to ensure that they will return to make any needed repairs.

Your last resort, if a contractor will not return, is to bring suit in civil court for breach of contract. Hire someone else to do the repair, and file a claim against the original contractor for the cost. Document the problem, and call the contractor who did the job. Take pictures, and keep a log of all phone calls. Whoever answers the phone, ask the person's name, and record the day and time of the call. Send the contractor a written request by certified mail, return receipt requested. Send copies to your attorney. Constantly follow up to make sure all the required work is completed. It is your responsibility to notify the contractors of problems to minimize any further damage to the system or the property. It is the contractors' responsibility to correct problems to minimize further damage.

Make copies of all transactions for your files. If the repairs are completed satisfactorily and in a timely manner, don't hold up the contractors' money. If they have done the work, pay them.

Now it's really done. Congratulations! Have another drink and celebrate. You have accomplished a difficult task, creating a one-of-a-kind home that is truly yours. It's time to enjoy it.

Now it's really done. Congratulations! Have another drink and celebrate.

INDEX

INDEX

I

Improvements, 11, 65–67, 73
Inspection requirements
    documents, 212–213
    for house, 210–212, 214
Inspectors
    bank, 200–201
    building, 91, 149, 200, 211–213
    and construction delays, 208
    electrical, 202, 212
    health department, 201
    insurance, 201
    relationship with, 198–200
Insulated sheathing, 113
Insulation
    cellulose, 114
    fiberglass, 112, 115
    requirements, 112–113
    R-values, 112–113, 115
    sheathing, 113
    and ventilation, 114–115
    windows and doors, 115–116
Insurance, 138–139, 218–219
Interest-only loans, 86
Interest rates, 153–156
    caps on, 156
    teaser, 158–159

K

Kiln-dried lumber, 182

L

Land titles, 68–69
Lenders
    and construction delays, 208–209
    dealing with, 147–148
    types of, 3–4
Lien release or affidavit, 133, 135
Liens, 80, 82
Living space, 43
Loan packages, 86, 147–151
Loans
    80-percent, 11–12
    95-percent, 11, 151

adjustable-rate, 17
bridge, 160
closing, 15, 86
construction, 17, 85, 149–150
conventional, 10–11, 15, 16
fees for, 150–151
interest-only, 86
low-interest, 12
separate from personal funds, 161–162
structuring, 149–151
using less cash, 17–19
    See also Mortgages
Loan-to-value ratio, 10
Lots. *See* Building lots
Lumber, 113, 182–183

M

Management company, 133, 135, 213
Market value, 11, 143
Mason, 108
Materials
    damaged or defective, 195–196
    for framing, 182–183
    ordering, 168–169
    tracking deliveries of, 195–196
Mechanic's liens, 133
Mortgage advertising, 158–159
Mortgage banker, 3–4, 9
Mortgage bond, 16, 220–222
Mortgage broker, 3–4, 9
Mortgage insurance, 17–18
Mortgage note, 16, 220–221
Mortgages
    adjustable-rate, 17, 153, 156–157
    amortization, 152
    annual percentage rate (APR), 154–156
    balloon, 158
    definition, 16, 151
    first, 19, 158
    fixed-rate, 152–153, 156–157
    foreclosure, 19, 157
    interest adjustment, 223–224
    interest rates, 14–15, 94
    packaging, 9–11

INDEX

Surveyors, 27–28
Survey stake, 166

T
Take-out loan, 17
Tax maps, 61–62
Tile installer, 117
Titles, 68–69, 78, 80, 133
Title settlement statement, 220
Total package price, 10–11
Trim installer, 117
Trusses, 184–185

U
Underbidding, 118
U.S. Department of Housing and Urban
    Development (HUD), 102

V
Ventilation, 114–115

W
Warranties, 224
Water table, 56–57, 63, 170–171
Wells, 63, 170–171
    dry, 173
Windows and doors, 115–116
Workmanship, poor, 207

Z
Zoning laws, 70–72, 166–168
Zoning variance, 71–72, 168